# SPIRITUALITY OF ADULT EDUCATION AND TRAINING

The Professional Practices in Adult Education and Human Resource Development Series explores issues and concerns of practitioners who work in the broad range of settings in adult and continuing education and human resource development.

The books are intended to provide information and strategies on how to make practice more effective for professionals and those they serve. They are written from a practical viewpoint and provide a forum for instructors, administrators, policy makers, counselors, trainers, managers, program and organizational developers, instructional designers, and other related professionals.

Michael W. Galbraith
Editor-in-Chief

# SPIRITUALITY OF ADULT EDUCATION AND TRAINING

Leona M. English
Tara J. Fenwick
Jim Parsons

KRIEGER PUBLISHING COMPANY
MALABAR, FLORIDA
2003

Original Edition 2003

Printed and Published by
**KRIEGER PUBLISHING COMPANY**
**KRIEGER DRIVE**
**MALABAR, FLORIDA 32950**

**Library of Congress Cataloging-in-Publication Data**

English, Leona M.
    Spirituality of adult education and training / Leona M. English,
Tara J. Fenwick, Jim Parsons. — Original ed.
        p.   cm. — (The professional practices in adult education and
        human resource development series)
    Includes bibliographical references and index.
    ISBN 1-57524-180-3 (hardcover : alk. paper)
    1. Teaching—Religious aspects. 2. Spiritual life. 3. Adult education—
Philosophy. 4. Employees—Training of—Philosophy. I. Fenwick, Tara J.
II. Parsons, James (James B.) III. Title. IV. Series.
LB1027.2 .E54 2003
374'.001—dc21                                                    2002027572

10   9   8   7   6   5   4   3   2

# CONTENTS

# PREFACE

This book gives voice to the many ways in which spirituality intersects with the lives of adult educators and trainers. If you are an adult educator or trainer who is interested in acknowledging and highlighting the spiritual dimensions of your teaching, this book is for you. We invite you to find an idea here that sparks your interest, challenges your assumptions, or suggests a new way of approaching your practice. We have included stories and exercises to help you.

We begin by providing a broad overview of spirituality, making a case for the importance of spirituality in the lives of adults generally. In Chapter 1, Introducing Spirituality, we locate spirituality within the context of adult education and training. We define spirituality and argue the need for a common language and definition of the term. The history of early adult education movements such as Chautauqua, Antigonish, Highlander, and Mondragon is used to show the original spiritual purpose. We develop the argument that the fields of adult education and training need to recover some of their early concerns for holistic, spiritually informed, and socially responsible practice.

In Chapter 2, Reconciling Difference: Different Dimensions and Approaches to Spirituality, we review and classify current research and theory in spirituality as it relates to adult education and training. We present a framework along with analytic tools for exploring similarities and differences in the most prominent writings in spirituality. Current issues arising in ethics for various professions, the increasing societal emphasis on community, and the new focus on caring and relationships are explored in terms of spiritual perspectives.

In Chapter 3, Developing Our Spirituality, we encourage adult educators and trainers to foster their own spirituality as a basis for integrating spirituality into their practice. We demonstrate the use of journals, reflective reading, artwork, soul friends, and body movement as means of developing spirituality. In Chapter 4, Spirituality in the Work of the Educator and Trainer, we turn our attention to teaching in order to discuss the ways that spirituality moves in education and training practice, and show the tensions and dilemmas of promoting spirituality as a part of andragogy/pedagogy. We examine the following:

- Ways educators can cultivate learning environments as sacred spaces
- Strategies for teaching holistically—valuing the spiritual
- Teacher-learner relationships
- The use of mentoring and coaching as spiritual activities
- Development of programs in spirituality
- Ethics and the educator/trainer—developing spirituality-based frames for ethical choices

This chapter faces head-on the fears that practitioners have about spirituality in their work world, and discusses them in depth.

In Chapter 5, Spirituality in the Workplace, we focus on how spirituality can be incorporated into workplace education. We provide examples of spirituality as part of explicit worker development in corporate settings: one example illustrates questionable ethics and confusing outcomes, whereas the other shows an attempt to authentically promote the well-being of participants. Readers are invited to debate ideological and political issues in both cases.

In Chapter 6, Adult Educators and Trainers as Leaders of Change, we conclude the discussion and show how the full acknowledgment and integration of spirituality in adult education and training can change the field. We suggest ways that adult educators and trainers can engage in that process. Finally, we provide suggestions for further reading.

Throughout the chapters, all three of us write from our

own experiences within particular spiritualities which must be acknowledged. It so happens that each one of us has journeyed through a Christian spirituality, although we have followed very different paths located in three very different (and contested) orientations. So, this is what we know best and what we believe. At the same time, we have been inspired and enlightened by friends and writers devoutly rooted in traditions different from our own. And while we cannot pretend to slip out of our own positionalities to present some neutral or transcendent vision of spirituality, we do believe there is a common space available where all spiritual seekers may gather and commune, for purposes of enriching their beliefs and their lives.

We anticipate a number of audiences for this book. One is individual academics teaching in community colleges or universities in various disciplines related to adult education and training. These include adult and higher education, medical and nursing education, leadership and organizational development, and ethics. The current literature shows growing interest in spiritual dimensions of practice among almost all educators.

Another audience is individual practitioners, including trainers/facilitators and program planners/coordinators in human resources development situated in business, government, and consulting firms. This group also includes practitioners in professional continuing education, including faculty development programs at various institutions. Current literature demonstrates the increasing emphasis on incorporating spirituality in these contexts.

Graduate students of adult education and training may find this book useful, as may adult religious educators of various faith traditions and denominations. The audience also includes graduate students studying Christian education in seminaries and theological colleges across North America.

We recognize the complexity of spirituality. We have attempted to highlight the benefits and challenges of incorporating spirituality in our practice. It is our hope the readers will engage our ideas and suggestions, and will use them to strengthen adult education and training.

# ACKNOWLEDGMENTS

The authors wish to offer a sincere thanks to Mary Roberts and Michael Galbraith at Krieger Publishing for believing in this project and helping them see it through to completion.

**From Leona M. English:**
A special thanks to my sisters, Virginia English and Nora English, who provided a listening ear and an abundance of faith in me. I acknowledge, too, my colleagues at St. Francis Xavier University, who always managed to appear fascinated by my many tangents while doing this project. I am grateful to the Father Gatto Fund at St. Francis Xavier University for providing partial research support for this book. Most of all, I thank Tara and Jim, coauthors, who made this book possible.

**From Tara J. Fenwick:**
Many thanks to Dr. Terry Fossen, an extraordinary spiritual mentor, and to the many students whose challenges have helped refine my thinking about spirituality. I am very grateful for Leona's vision and persistence and Jim's patient eye for detail.

**From Jim Parsons:**
I wish to thank my grandfather, long since departed, for helping me see how to live as a Christian in love with the world; my Department of Secondary Education and Faculty of Education at the University of Alberta for letting me work in the area of my passion. I would love to acknowledge my coauthors, whose work has been nothing short of inspiring—not often does one write with a team of people so knowledgeable or easy to work with. I thank them.

# THE AUTHORS

**Leona M. English** is associate professor of adult education at St. Francis Xavier University in Antigonish, Nova Scotia. She holds a B.A. (1984) and B.Ed. (1984) from Memorial University of Newfoundland; an M.R.E. (1989) from St. Michael's College, University of Toronto; and an Ed.D. (1994) from Teachers College, Columbia University. She has taught at the Atlantic School of Theology and St. Michael's College, University of Toronto. English's areas of research are in adult learning: international education spirituality, mentoring, informal learning, and journal writing. Her publications include *Mentoring in Religious Education* (1998), *Addressing the Spiritual Dimensions of Adult Learning* (2000, with Marie Gillen), and *Promoting Journal Writing in Adult Education* (2001, with Marie Gillen). She is an active member of the Association of Professors and Researchers in Religious Education.

**Tara J. Fenwick** is an assistant professor of adult education at the University of Alberta in Edmonton, Alberta, and adjunct professor for St. Stephen's Theological College also in Edmonton.

**Jim Parsons** has been a professor in the Department of Secondary Education at the University of Alberta for 27 years. He has published over 50 books in his areas of study: religious education and social studies education. Besides teaching at the University of Alberta, he has taught Christian education at Edmonton Baptist Seminary and Concordia Lutheran Seminary. Currently he is an advisor for graduate students in a program on moral and religious education housed at the University of Alberta.

# CHAPTER 1

## Introducing Spirituality

Perhaps you thought you were living in a highly secularized society. Think again. Browse an airport bookstore. Read the business section of any large newspaper. Attend a conference in adult education or training. You will bump into more spirits than Scrooge saw in a single evening. Spurred partly by popular culture's interest and partly by an interest in returning to a concern for the common good, spirituality in adult education and training is an emerging topic. There is a stirring inside, and adult educators and trainers are responding by meditating aloud upon their own spirituality and bringing this spirituality to bear in their teaching and learning encounters. The purpose of this book is to focus directly on spirituality and explore many ways in which adult education and training are affected by it.

This interest in spirituality is not confined to adult educators and trainers. In an international bestseller, an ordinary 14-year-old girl named Sophie Amundsen, who lives with her mother in an ordinary Norwegian suburb, receives an unsigned letter in the mail with only a three-word question: who are you? (Gaarder, 1994). In a while, another anonymous note arrives, asking: where did the world come from? Finally, Sophie receives a three-page unsigned letter—her first lesson in a course on the history of philosophy. Gaarder, the Norwegian high school teacher who wrote *Sophie's World*: *A Novel About the History of Philosophy* is amazed that his beginner's guide to philosophy, addressing what are essentially spiritual questions, became a runaway bestseller. It has also been published in China, Germany, Italy, Japan, and South Korea. The first English edition, even with mixed reviews, sold out its first 50,000 copies in less than two weeks.

A report in the *New York Times Magazine* points out that 96% of the population believe in God, 90% turn to God in prayer, and that 40% of Americans and 38% of Canadians attend a weekly religious service of some sort. More than 87% of Americans claim to be Christian; 2% Jewish, and the remainder Buddhist, Muslim, or other (Shorto, 1997). An undisclosed number are drawn to new age spiritualities (Ó Murchú, 1998). Yet, we still do not know exactly why people are drawn to these beliefs and practices. We suspect it is because people are on a quest to make meaning from their lives and their work.

We also believe this same spirituality movement is permeating adult education and training. The frequency of publications using various spiritual perspectives to examine adult learning and pedagogy is increasing (e.g., Dillard, Abdur-Rashid & Tyson, 2000; MacPherson, 1996; Tisdell, 2000b). Workplace educators have also been working for some time to find ways to connect spirituality with their practice, in what Conlin (1999) describes as a "spiritual revival sweeping across Corporate America." Neal (1997), a professor of management education at New Haven University exploring the new focus on spirituality in organizations, attributes it to baby boomers. They have approached the reflective years of middle age at a time of intoxicating changes and frightening challenges to old rules defining family, success, truth and "the good."

Other workplace educators have revealed similar interests. Perhaps the word *interest* is too tame. There has been an explosion of organizational training materials concerned with spirituality (Finlayson, 1997; Lee & Zemke, 1993; Leigh, 1997) and another large group of spiritual management development books (Kleiner, 1996; Secretan, 1996; Zukav, 1990). Organizational training is not the only area being blasted by this explosion. Even the rather historically stodgy area of curriculum theory has seen an increase in texts acknowledging the significance of spirituality in learning and teaching (Pinar, Reynolds, & Taubman, 1995; Slattery, 1995); and higher education texts presenting teaching approaches of the heart (Apps, 1996; Palmer, 1983, 1998).

On a continent whose history has embraced the separation of church and state as the rule of the day—either through legislation (the United States) or lethargy (Canada)—the growth of books of the spirit over the past decade and the intertwining of these books into the fabric of institutional North American life are surprising. Perhaps the most surprised are the people who wrote them. Possibly even Redfield (1993) did not predict that his *The Celestine Prophesy* would become a bestseller, let alone develop a cult following. Spiritual books of varying rigor and quality have become continuing bestsellers, everything from James Hillman's *The Soul's Code* (1996) to Gary Zukav's *The Seat of the Soul* (1990). And who can forget that the very first Chicken Soup book was for nothing less than—the Soul (Canfield & Hansen, 1993).

The attention that spirituality receives in the public press may be indicative of a universal need to name and embrace spiritual concepts and issues. Adult educators and trainers themselves feel a need to bring this too long left-at-home concept to their workplace and to explore it with the learners with whom they are working. The profession and practice of adult education and training cannot hold with the strict divisions between personal and professional that has led to a wrenching divide within us. Spirituality is the greatest issue facing us, and it commands our attention and that of our learners. It is time for educators to give more attention to the issue of spirituality.

## TEACHING AND MAKING
## DECISIONS WITH INTEGRITY

We believe that the most straightforward way to promote a spiritual dimension in teaching and learning is to make a deliberate attempt to think and act ethically. Almost every daily decision in the learning environment has an ethical component.

Teachers can also raise deliberate and provocative questions that spark conversation and evoke comments from learners.

These common activities are the heart of ethical teaching because they are based on those choices and decisions fundamental to teaching and learning. These ethical choices center on decisions about the boundaries that constitute pedagogical relationships, about the nature of the spirit within the exercise of teaching, and about the real reason spirituality is being incorporated. These activities necessarily include making thoughtful decisions and weighing decisions against how they help the environment, the people in the corporation, and the learners. Ethical choices implicitly include a basic recognition of the person as spiritual. This means making ethical choices throughout the whole activity of education, including choices about how we educate learners and choices about how we involve learners in decisions.

All spiritual traditions are concerned with questions of morality. What actions are moral—what actions are right or wrong—in terms of both intent and implications? Western traditions seem more concerned with intent; Eastern traditions include a consideration of the responsibility of the impact of an action that transcends questions of what an individual hoped to do. And, questions of right and wrong link personal decisions about the different ways to act with the groundings of one's spiritual belief. Few spiritual traditions would not seek a consistency between belief and behavior.

Morality is often linked to one's understanding of the nature of the spirit and the spiritual universe, the meaning of life, the purpose of the spiritual journey, and the "right response" to spiritual pursuits. There are key distinctions among the ethical systems of different spiritual traditions. An issue for adult educators and trainers centers on how these different frameworks, based on these ethical systems, can be useful. A specific question is how to deal with pluralistic moral stances in making ethical choices in a diverse community of learners.

*Ethics, of course, is not something that adults get from reading a book or from being told right from wrong. It*

*takes considerable thought on one's part to find ways to be
ethical and to do the right thing. It does not happen in a
moment, but rather over the course of a lifetime. Consider
the words of Dag Hammarskjöld, a Swede and former sec-
retary general of the United Nations, whose diary,* Markings *(1964), was published after his death. He said, "I don't
know Who—or what—put the question. I don't know
when it was put. I don't even remember answering. But at
some moment I did answer Yes to someone or something
and from that hour I was certain that existence is meaningful and that, therefore, my life, in self-surrender, had a
goal." (p. 169)*

## WHAT IS SPIRITUALITY?

Before we go further, however, we believe it is important
to explore what we mean by spirituality. Part of the power of
spirituality is its many rich layers, meanings, and expressions.
Early 20th century adult educator Basil Yeaxlee (1925), who
had a long involvement with the YMCA, saw spirituality as syn-
onymous with religion. However in today's postmodern plural-
ism, it may seem impossible to even begin to describe spirituality
in ways that would obtain approval by different groups. As we
sequestered ourselves in Park City, Utah, to complete the manu-
script for this book, we visited a bookstore almost completely
devoted to the topic of spirituality where there were—to our
count—38 different categories for the spiritual. Here is the
list: tarot, oracles, channeled, death-dying, meditation, chakras,
women-goddesses, men-gods (a small section), spirituality, consciousness, right-livelihood (the bookstore attendant could not
explain this category), self-empowerment, uncovering, personal
experience, new physics, prophecy, past lives, tantra, relationships, sexuality, eastern wisdom, zen, tao, astrology (the largest
unit with six shelves of books), ceremony, celtic, mythology,
gaia, shamanism, crystals, ancient wisdom, Native American,
angels-fairies, divine child, family, feng shui, inspiration, and
guided imagery. As unusual as some may seem, we must assume

that every one of these topics is authentic and meaningful to someone.

Whatever it is, spirituality has certainly, in the past 75 years, grown either larger than (or safer than) a focus on religion. Fenwick and Lange (1998) describe spirituality, in part, as "a yearning to connect with a community, a higher power, or a transcendent energy—and to liberate this energy within one's self" (p. 64). Building on this understanding of spirituality as broader than religion, and spirituality as both inner- and outer-directed, English and Gillen (2000a) define spirituality as "an awareness of something greater than ourselves. . . . [that] moves one *outward* to others as an expression of one's spiritual experiences" (p. 1).

Such a broad definition represents a secular or public spirituality (Berry, 1988), as distinguished from religious spirituality. This broad definition also guides the development of this book and reflects our belief that, if one is to understand the current impact of spirituality, one's definition should be as inclusive as possible while embedding a sense of movement, relationship, and mystery. The concept should be broadly defined and accept many authentic expressions.

Attempting to define spirituality is problematic. The attempt presumes that the experience of spirituality can be captured in words, its meaning contained, and its essence identified. Part of our goal in this book is to encourage readers to think about what spirituality means in their own lives; what practices or rituals they have to nurture their spirituality; and what challenges them about spiritual practice. If this can happen in a serious way, it almost doesn't matter how one categorizes a book on a bookstore shelf.

*Spirituality is as timeless as humanity. Fourteenth-century anchorite Julian of Norwich spent her days praying and meditating in her cell, which was attached to the wall of the St. Julian's Church, a cathedral in Norwich, England. She received 16 showings or revelations of God and recorded them in a book called* The Showings. *In this collection she records what the Divine tells her: "All will be well, and every kind of thing will be well" (p. 225). Seven centuries later T. S. Eliot (1944) used these very words in his Four Quartets.*

## ASSUMPTIONS ABOUT THE SPIRITUALITY OF EDUCATION AND TRAINING

Many assumptions undergird the concept of spirituality, as we discuss in this book. One assumption is that education and training are about more than the bottom line. Education is about giving meaning to life and to living and, first and foremost, assisting the growth of the human spirit. Such a philosophical grounding will help trainers increase organizational productivity and profit. The goal is to help adults to grow and live abundantly as active participants in their communities and workplaces.

The second assumption is that spirituality is about more than religion, though these two terms may be connected. As others such as Wuthnow (1998) have pointed out, spirituality may or may not have an institutional or religious form. Spirituality may indeed be about finding meaning in relationships, or work itself, or in oneself. Though we acknowledge that religious activities such as meditation training and formalized Bible studies have been useful in some educational and workplace environments, this again is not the thrust we promote in this book. We are interested in deepening the meaning and quality of people's learning, without focusing on any particular religious traditions.

The third assumption is that adults enact their spiritual side in a variety of ways. For some, this spiritual dimension is reflected in overt religious connections. For others, spirituality is part of a lifelong search for meaning or a quest to make sense of everyday routines. For others, spiritual disciplines such as meditation, bodywork, or spiritual reading are part of everyday activities. Whatever the individual expression, we believe the spiritual dimension of adulthood, adult education, and training needs to be recognized, honored, and fostered in educational settings, whether in postsecondary institutions, community-based education, or the workplace.

## FOUR KEY IDEAS ABOUT SPIRITUALITY

This book is based on four key ideas about spirituality and its relationship to adult education and training.

### Spirituality Is an Integral Part of the Fabric of Adult Education and Training

Spirituality is not new to adult education, even if writing about it may be. What educators and trainers need, we believe, is a common definition for the term *spirituality* that is inclusive of all adults and that supports the pedagogical purposes of the encounters between educators and learners. The work of adult educators and trainers necessarily puts them in daily contact with adult needs to make spiritual meaning of life. The history of early adult education movements discussed later in this chapter highlights this original spiritual purpose and the deep roots of spirituality in our field. Celebrated adult education leaders from Bishop Grundtvig (Danish folk schools) to Moses Coady exemplify pedagogical practice springing directly from spirituality.

### Spiritual Practices Can Be Fostered

Spirituality can be seen through a number of different lenses. Learners and educators have their own perspectives. It is possible for adult educators and trainers to cultivate their own spirituality through purposeful reflection, journal writing, reflective reading, artwork, music, body movement, and other practices. We invite educators to make spaces for the holy within their busy lives. We also invite educators to consider weaving their spirituality into their vocation. They can then communicate this personal integration of spirituality into their interactions with adult learners.

## Spirituality Challenges the Work of the Educator and Trainer

Recognizing and fostering the practice of spirituality in adult education and training can cause tensions and dilemmas. Promoting spirituality as part of pedagogy requires a knowledge of how to engage in spiritual practices, including cultivating classrooms as sacred spaces and teaching holistically. (Later in this book we will discuss fears of this integration at length.)

## Spirituality Has Value for Workplace Education

Spirituality has the potential to improve conditions of work and the generative potential of the workplace, supporting the well-being of workers at a time when many report feeling frazzled and fragmented by work. This focus on well-being has multiple benefits for the organization and its people. It can highlight the invisible and incorporate spirituality into adult education and training in ethical and meaningful ways.

## BRIDGING THE GAP BETWEEN THE PERSONAL AND THE PROFESSIONAL

Spirituality intersects the personal and professional, and makes most sense when it is integrated fully into all aspects of a person's life. Consequently, spirituality is gaining prominence as an integral part of adult development theory. Clark and Caffarella (1999) included spirituality in their four-part classification of adult development theory: biological, psychological, sociocultural, and integrative. They situate spirituality as integrative. For them, this means that spirituality is part of all the others—not totally psychological, biological, social, or cultural.

Instead, it is an amalgam of all these. In her chapter in the book, Tisdell (1999a) observes that spirituality is "all encompassing and cannot be torn from other aspects of adult development" (p. 94).

Given that spirituality is a part of life stage and other adult development theory, spiritual elements are an integral part of a holistic approach to learning. Similarly, transformative learning theory, theories of cognition, and experiential learning theories are linked to writings on spirituality. Dirkx's (1997) notion of the soul in education points to the importance of recognizing and honoring the spiritual in learning.

The complexity of the postmodern world makes it important that educators and trainers address spirituality. Building on the work of Spretnak, Moules (2000) argues that there is room within the postmodern framework for spirituality. Although postmodern thought arches toward individuality and particularity, spirituality can complement this thrust by bringing healing and connectedness. As Moules points out, "Postmodernism does not have to be about disconnection" (p. 7). Adult educators and trainers can, by bringing spirituality into their practice, find ways to approach the common while honoring the particular.

To us, one thing is clear. The popular interest in spirituality in North America is definitely increasing rather than passing in importance. In adult education and training literature, spirituality has emerged as a serious subject for theory and practice within the past decade. Writers in adult education have identified a mass search for meaning among adults (Merriam & Heuer, 1996), some of which is part of the innate search for meaning and purpose in life Martin Buber described a half century ago. Spiritual yearning is universal and timeless.

As Slattery (1995) notes, our age's appetite for material consumption has produced dissatisfaction, despair, and anxiety. Globalizing forces, glittering images, and technological change sweep over us even faster than they did last year. The result? An increasing human hunger to understand and experience spirituality. What makes our age differ from the past is that many are seeking spiritual wholeness through adult education and training, formal and informal, rather than through traditional religious practice (O Murchú, 1998).

We believe adult educators and trainers are wise to examine the facets of spirituality directly useful for their own practice. As they work to make pedagogical choices, they may need rigorous comparative perspectives and frameworks to help them take stock and synthesize the vast array of emerging spiritual theory and practice. Some may need help to make sense of the spiritual dimensions of their own lives, the spiritual needs of learners, and the implications for their roles as educators and trainers. Not unlike the learners they work with, educators might need a little connecting spirituality with the roots, existing theory, and goals of the field of adult education and training.

> *Bringing spirituality to our work requires what the Vietnamese poet and Zen master Thich Nhat Hanh (1990) calls mindfulness. He suggests that we exercise mindfulness even when driving a car, suggesting that when we get into a car, we be mindful of where we are, what is happening as we move, and that just as the car moves quickly, we also move quickly. This mindfulness is about being present to what we are doing, about being centered and not flustered in our daily activities. Hahn reminds us that we need to be present to the driving and not spend our time trying to get there. He also lives as if life is now, in what we are doing, not in the future or the arrival point. Everything we do ought to bring us to the present moment—this is mindfulness.*

## THE ROOTS OF SPIRITUALITY IN ADULT EDUCATION AND TRAINING

Spirituality has long been part of, and the motivation for, adult education and training practice. Some of the most significant social movements in adult education began with a spiritual impulse, often spurred on by Gospel values. New York's Chautauqua, Nova Scotia's Antigonish, and Spain's Mondragon all have religious and/or spiritual roots. We believe the field of adult education and training would do well to recover some of the early concerns of the field for spiritually informed practice and socially responsible adult education and training. These have never really disappeared from our practice as adult educators and trainers. We must simply come to recognize them when they are present. We do not mean that adult education and training should return to religiously based practice. But, we do mean that adult education and training should embrace its spiritual roots of passion and social action directed to the common good.

Historian Gordon Selman (1998) reminds us how many adult educators have had religious or spiritual roots. He observes that early adult educators were very much connected with social justice and reform movements. He highlights the Antigonish Movement, founded on Christian principles and specifically on an ideology that everyone could be free and independent masters of their own destiny (Coady, 1939). The Antigonish Movement was a socioeconomic movement to organize miners and fishers in eastern Nova Scotia into cooperatives and credit unions, and to move them away from dependence and servitude (Gillen, 1998). Historically, adult educators and trainers were interested in change and improvement in society as part of the common good and as part of one's social and spiritual responsibility. That interest seems to be reemerging.

Selman's (1998) observations are borne out by a brief look at some other early North American practitioners. For instance, Myles Horton taught Bible school for the Presbyterian Church in Tennessee and in his youth attended New York City's liberal Union Theological Seminary. In an interview with Union Theological Seminary professor William Bean Kennedy (1981), Horton discusses his connections with church and the Gospel, and how he was influenced by 20th century theological giants such as Reinhold Neibuhr and Harry F. Ward. Horton's wife and colleague, Aimee Horton, was similarly involved with the Quakers and was a human rights activist. Together they supported social change initiatives, including organizing interracial meetings for the YMCA.

Other examples of spiritually based adult education and training activities include Chautauqua which was founded in upstate New York at the turn of the 20th century to improve teaching in Sunday schools, and which continues to feature spiritual study as a central part of its educational programs. Other early adult educators such as Eduard Lindeman (1921) wrote works such as *The Community* addressed specifically to a Christian audience. In this book, Lindeman reflected on the social gospel themes of "the kingdom and democracy, of the importance of a collective effort, of the critical role of science — of advocacy on behalf of the common person, and of the necessity to work on behalf of social change" (Fisher, 1997, p. 5). Fisher makes a convincing case that Lindeman's involvement in the YMCA, the Congregational Church, and the extension movement affected and influenced his writing. Fisher notes that at one point, Lindeman even gave lectures in honor of the leading social gospel theologian, Walter Rauschenbusch.

These early U.S. movements were coupled with a common interest internationally. In 1925, Basil Yeaxlee (1925) promoted the spiritual dimensions of adult education in his writing and professional work with the YMCA in Britain. For Yeaxlee there was no question: adult education was animated by spirituality. As well, the temperance movements of the early part of this century were, by and large, adult education movements with a strong religious basis (Lander, 2000b). Significantly, the Young Men's Christian Association (YMCA) has been a major employer of adult educators and trainers over the years. Lindeman once worked for them, as did Horton, Yeaxlee, and Corbett. Each was influenced directly by a religious upbringing to integrate social justice to his work in adult education. The separation of church and state was not as pronounced among them as it is for adult educators and trainers today.

Outside North America, the Mondragon program in Spain grew to be the most successful and ongoing cooperative movement in the world. It was founded by Father José Arizmendi as an extension of his Christian beliefs (MacLeod, 1997). Father José, a resistor to Franco in the Spanish Civil War, first established a small elementary technical school. With graduates of this school, he then founded a small worker-owned and -managed factory named ULGOR. At Mondragon they manufacture industrial and home appliances, as well as operate a credit union. This remains one of the largest worker-owned and -operated businesses in the world today.

In Brazil, Paulo Freire, perhaps the most cited and revered educator of the last half of the 20th century, not only had strong cultural and religious roots but saw his work as being spiritual. Lange (1998) and Welton (1993) each have discussed this spiritual influence, noting that Freire was deeply influenced by liberation theology in Latin America. Welton has specifically probed the intersections between Freire's conscientization and the Christian notion of conversion, linking Freire's ideas of freedom from oppression to the Gospel narrative. Not surprisingly, much of Freire's working life was spent with the World Council of Churches and with the Catholic University in São Paulo. Freire (1984) himself tells how he was spurred by his Christian faith to work for what he called an education for liberation.

A collection of essays on early Canadian adult educators (Rouillard, 1952) documents a strong and enduring connection with organized religion as a motivator for much of their educational work. This collection compiles the life stories of individuals working in sectors of education that no longer have strong ties to adult education and training, so narrow has the field become. The twelve educators profiled were leaders and founders in sectors as diverse as home economics, women's institutes, libraries, and universities. This book, *Pioneers of Adult Education in Canada,* contains essays originally written for the Canadian Association for Adult Education (CAAE) publication *Food for Thought.* These essays are filled with examples of the influence of organized religion and a thirst for justice in the lives of people such as Adelaide Hoodless, founder of the Women's Institutes, who later became president of the local YWCA, and Ned Corbett, a one-time theology student who founded Canadian farm radio and who later became president of the CAAE.

As leaders in the Antigonish movement, Moses Coady and Jimmy Tompkins's church affiliation is also detailed, as is the early instruction that cooperative organizer A. B. MacDonald received from Tompkins at St. Francis Xavier University. As a student of religion in Jimmy Tompkins's class, A. B. learned "economics with a religious bias" (Corbett, 1952, p. 96). As A. B. remembered it, Tompkins had his students read a book called *Key to the World Progress*, obviously not a typical religious book of the day. That his texts were provocative suggests that his classes were exciting and inspiring places to be. Not noted in Rouillard's book are the women of the Antigonish movement, most notably Delores Donnelly and Marie Michael MacKinnon, women religious who were active in promoting libraries as vehicles for adult education and community development (R. Neal, 1998). Their connections to Catholicism, and more specifically to a committed life as women religious, obviously influenced their motives.

Further information on the religious/spiritual/justice influences on the early adult education and training movement can be found in Welton's (1987) edited book *Knowledge for the People*. For instance, Alfred Fitzpatrick, founder of Frontier College, started as a Presbyterian missionary. He initiated a Canadian literacy movement in which teachers went to work alongside their students, working with and teaching railroad employees on the frontier. One of Fitzpatrick's first placements was among "loggers in the California Redwoods and in the Algoma District of northern Ontario" (Cook, 1987, pp. 36–37). However, Fitzpatrick "soon saw the futility of attempting to minister to men's spirits without first attending to their social needs" (p. 37). His work in founding Frontier College was directly inspired by his need to be of Christian service in the camps.

Religious educators are not surprised by the links of spirituality to adult education and training, though that knowledge is shared by few outside narrowly defined religious circles. Religious educators and theologians have long known Freire's own theological convictions and have claimed him as an inspiration for their work. For instance, Groome, the prominent religious educator and professor at Boston College, adapted Freire's work to create a five-part model for teaching Christian religious education. Groome's work, especially his now-classic *Christian Religious Education*, is used extensively in religious education in North America today.

There is a predominance of Christian stories here, perhaps because of the predominance of Christianity in the West. No doubt the majority of the world has as many or more stories, although they are not as accessible to North Americans. Yet, this deliberate reliance on Christianity has declined in recent years. In part, we are reluctantly cynical to name religion as important; but, more significantly our faith in organized religion has decreased (Shorto, 1997). In the West especially, we have moved from a more homogenous society, where religious tradition was a dominant part of community life and therefore education, to our post-Fordist workplaces and anxiety-laden techno-dazzle pop culture. Although our educational mythologies claim a generalized distrust of grand narratives, specifically with the promises of religion (English & Gillen, 2000b), in truth we live in a world driven by "keeping-up-with," which may be best seen in relation to communication technologies, a belief system of its own that infers some baselines of belief. We may be as religious as ever, even if the gods we worship have morphed. Whereas many schools and universities had Christian beginnings, this connection is generally fading as faith in organized religion and its promises has faded. Yet, the existential quest of humans to find meaning and to create meaning remains—this is eternal and is emerging now in the guise of spirituality and a commitment to the common good.

Matters of the spirit continue to interest people, even within adult education and training. Jarvis and Walters (1993) had no less than 19 authors contribute to their edited book *Adult Education and Theological Interpretations*. This book is a collection of essays on the connections between theology and adult education. The authors argue that both disciplines are about understanding human experience and finding personal and communal meaning in life, and the chapter authors have intersecting interests in both adult education and theology. In her contribution to that book, Clark, a feminist and former nun, notes, "When I began my doctoral studies in adult education I was struck by the number of people in the field with theological backgrounds" (p. 20). She herself worked in the church for 15 years.

Clark (1999) is not alone. Another feminist adult educator, Tisdell (2000a) discusses the social and cultural influences on her feminism. She points out that it was in a Jesuit school of theology that she first came to understand feminism. This interest led her into pastoral and chaplaincy work in the Roman Catholic Church, and eventually to her present interests in spirituality and emancipatory adult education (see also Tisdell, 2000b).

## VARIETIES OF EXPRESSION

Spirituality manifests itself in contexts as diverse as health education, workplace education, higher education, and international development education. Health education, in particular, increasingly gives attention to the spirit (Miller, 2000). There is a growing understanding that effective health education encompasses and integrates both the spirit and the body. This understanding of the effect one has on the other has even translated to nursing education, resulting in such journals as *Human Caring*, that speak directly to the need to cultivate all aspects of the person (body, mind, spirit) in order for full human living. Our learning, our being, and our development are so complex that an exclusive emphasis on the mechanics of education (how to do things) is not sufficient for humans to come to know.

In higher education, similar attention is paid to spirituality (MacAulay, Hynes, Mahaffey, & Wright, 2000). Proponents lay claim to centuries' old traditions of educating the whole person and declare their desire to attend to the spiritual, emotional, cognitive, and physical dimensions of adults. Parker Palmer's books on spirituality and education have greatly influenced this movement. Palmer's *To Know as We Are Known* (1983) and his more recent *The Courage to Teach* (1998) examine the interior life and its effect on teaching practice. Neither book is a how-to manual; both attempt to promote a spiritual approach to education. In higher education, Beauchamp and Parsons's *Teaching from the Inside Out* (2000) is an introduction to spirit teaching (used in undergraduate education courses), stressing the importance of relationship, interpersonal connection, and mutual respect in teaching.

International development education and community development have seen a similar resurgence of interest in the spiritual dimensions of education. In the journal *Development and Practice,* Ver Beek (2000) argues that spirituality can no longer be a taboo in development education and urges the recovery of a spiritual approach. Despite obvious problematic linkages of religion and colonialism, Ver Beek sees a move afoot to recover the links between spirituality and education. The culture of silence that the absence of dialogue about spirituality and education creates in development practice is awkward, problematic, and ought to be addressed.

> *When former Czechoslovakian president Vaclav Havel (1992) penned his "Dream for Czechoslovakia" he articulated best the interplay of mind and being, of theory and practice, of ideas and actions that is envisaged in this book. Havel said that in all the years he spent in material production, he never felt that "my spirit, my intellect, my consciousness—in other words, what makes me a human person—was somehow determined by that. On the contrary, if I produced something, I produced it as a person— that is, a creature with a spirit and a conscious mastery of his own fate. It was the outcome of a decision made by my human 'I,' and, to a greater or lesser extent, that 'I' had to share in my material production." (p. 57)*

## SUMMARY

This chapter has presented our basic understandings and assumptions about spirituality in adult education and training. Adult education and training began with leaders who believed their very work was, in itself, spiritual. Our historical mentors did not separate their spiritual sides from their work. In fact, their spirituality animated their work and their educational practice lent direction and focus to their spirituality. Somewhere in the past fifty years adult education and training have become more about teaching techniques and learning styles than about inspiration, aspiration, and consecration. Separating the spiritual from the educational might be a safer approach to practice, but it is short-sighted in terms of human need and innate human understanding.

To us, there is a simple answer to the question "Why do we need a book like this?" As adult educators and trainers, we can no longer ignore the spiritual basis of our practice. The desire for holistic education may be a longing for spiritual solace, energy, and connection emanating from contemporary cultures. We believe that adult education and training should reconnect, wherever there is disconnection, the educational and the spiritual. To not do so would be both unnatural and misguided.

Spirituality is fast becoming big business in adult education and training. We hope to help adult educators and trainers think more clearly and critically about the possibilities of their work as a holistic, spiritual enterprise. Throughout the remainder of this book, we will attend more specifically to this enterprise. We have faith that our work will be a helpful addition to the field.

---

## STARTING POINTS FOR FURTHER REFLECTION

Not only do we see spirituality as something we incorporate into our work, we value the spirituality of the work itself. Spirituality is not only about quiet, retreats, and reflection; it is about the busy, noisy activity in our everyday lives. A spirituality of work is far different from a spirituality of contemplation.

Spirituality as a discipline needs to be practiced and integrated into daily routines. Before you launch into the rest of the book, we challenge you to begin thinking about whether spirituality simply is a part-time endeavor or a hobby for you or if it is an integral part of your everyday work and educational practice. Here are some questions that Pierce (1999) suggests we consider:

- Do you practice the discipline of doing your best work? This discipline means giving your adult education and training work your best effort. Although none of us ever do our jobs perfectly, we need to do our best, accept this, and then move on. Giving our all to our work means that we act responsibly and with integrity.
- Do you practice the discipline of balance? Work is only one part of your life as an educator or trainer. Balancing family, work, volunteer commitments, and other responsibilities is an important part of the spirituality of balance. Allowing one part of your life to rule produces an unhealthy person, unable to contribute well to society or to work.
- Do you practice the discipline of giving thanks and congratulations? This discipline is a way of recognizing other people's work and contributions to the workplace. Times of special achievement such as workplace anniversaries need to be honored and respected.
- Do you practice the discipline of deciding when enough is enough? This is the discipline of doing our best and not taking on everything handed to us. The workplace may never recognize this limit, but as individuals we need to.
- Do you practice the discipline of mindfulness? This is the discipline of paying full attention to what is happening in your work and relationships. Only by being present to the present can you be fully alive.

# CHAPTER 2

## Reconciling Difference: Different Dimensions and Approaches to Spirituality

Crucial questions flow from Chapter 1: How shall we choose among the many available spiritual traditions to ground our own practice of adult education or training? Do some ground our practice and ourselves "better," whatever "better" means? And, what are the implications of choosing one tradition over another? It is impossible to ignore the flowering of spirituality that seems to bloom throughout our world. Look around. New Age religions are growing alongside a rejuvenation and redefining of older traditions including Islam, Buddhism, Judaism, Roman Catholic and Protestant Christianity, Sufism, Hinduism, and African American spiritualities. At the same time as scholars note the postmodern breakdown of grand narratives, a revival and even a remarketing of ancient religions such as Kaballah, Celtic, North American Native and Earth Mother spiritual traditions are occurring.

The mystical and moral are increasingly combined with the intellectual and the scientific. The results are books and research filled with calls for transpersonal psychology, Jungian psychology, feminist scholarship, deep ecology and complexity theories of the new science (Casti, 1994, Waldrop, 1992). As Kung (1988), a Roman Catholic theologian, put it, "the intellectual crisis of our time is co-determined by a religious crisis" (p. 6). Taylor (1996) claims there is a wild explosion of spirituality in all phases of contemporary life. He believes this is unique to our particular period in history, and represents a rebellion against a "flat" world where things have become subordinated to utility and instrumentality. People are pushing for something fuller, deeper, and higher.

In Chapter 1, we suggested that a spiritual famine seems to exist in North American society. More to the interest of our work here, we suggest that it may exist in our own work in adult education and training. Many have lamented the predominant focus in recent decades of adult education on technique, procedure, and measurement (Collins, 1991) and the erosion of its spirit—what Collins calls "thoughtful ethical commitment" (p. 41). Some have shown that spiritually centered pedagogies have long characterized the practice of certain groups, such as African American women, whose voices have heretofore been hushed by mainstream academia (Dillard, Abdur-Rashid, & Tyson, 2000).

We may search for a quiet space to balance the frenetic pace and frightening contradictions of teaching, to reorder priorities so we might withstand the onslaught of images and reconnect with principles and traditions of wisdom that can simplify and endow our practice with deeper meaning. Palmer (1983) writes that beneath our brokenness is a desire to overcome disconnectedness from one's self, from human community, and from the earth. We seek to be plugged back in. But our fervent seeking often takes the form of consumptive spirituality, continuously grasping for more. We move relentlessly and restlessly from one communion to the next. Meanwhile, spiritual vendors and missionary merchants proliferate, and adults everywhere may be vulnerable to their hype. Spirituality suggests, even requires, that we suspend the critical rationality we ordinarily rely upon to protect us from falsehood and manipulation. Like sex, spirituality can be blissful, transcendent, and move us to more intimate and connective relationships. Or, it can be cruel, perverse, and even exploitative.

## DISTINGUISHING AMONG THE SPIRITUAL

With this in mind, the purpose of this chapter is to clarify and reconcile foundational dimensions of difference among spiritual traditions. While much of the literature we read invokes and even romanticizes the spiritual, we often pay insufficient attention to foundational beliefs and the blurred conceptual distinctions among these spiritual traditions. We should not.

*One of the most profound stories of how to determine authenticity is told in the Christian Scriptures. In the Book of Acts, the apostles are brought before the Jewish council, the Sanhedrin. They are charged with teaching in Jesus' name, despite the laws against it. The apostle Peter says they do what they do because they must obey God. The council becomes agitated and angry, until Gamaliel, a Pharisee and doctor of the Jewish law, defends the Apostles saying that if the teaching is of humans it will not last, but if it is of God, it will thrive. The Apostles are released. The lesson is that what is right, true, and authentic will thrive in the long run. What is false and shallow will die. The same test can be applied to spiritual movements. (Acts 5)*

Many spiritual writers now seem to draw freely from New Age literature, pop psychology, Western and Eastern religious doctrines and theology, recovery movement "healing" literature, and even personal ecstatic experience. Such eclecticism may be a consumer's or publisher's dream, but for the seekers of true spirituality this meshing of spiritual traditions can be confusing, misleading, and decentering. We may be left with profoundly contradictory, sometimes superficial responses and promises.

But, how are people to distinguish among vastly different spiritual beliefs to find a path that is right for themselves? A beginning would be the practice of discernment to understand the meaning of the spiritual in our learning process, in our relationships, and in our community. We need to move beyond shallow notions and romantic rhetoric to more rigorous conceptions of what spirituality is and what it means.

We define discernment as an awakening to see what is true, "a kind of critical reflection on the wellsprings and dynamics of our own thoughts and wishes, an examination of our dispositions, dealings, and deeper motives, with an eye to making solid judgments and good decisions" (Egan, 1996, p. 6). To discern means to examine our own desires and intentions, as well as to distinguish "what is deep from what is shallow, what is free from what is compulsive." Even "our boasts of virtue can be evasive mechanisms of defense, our zeal for truth can be the cover story for our lust to dominate" (p. 7). Discernment is a time-honored spiritual discipline that helps us engage our intuition and spiritual senses as well as our rationality. Its purpose is to explore the relations between our longings, souls, knowledge, power, purpose, life, the divine, and love.

But why should an adult educator or trainer waste time examining complex philosophical and theological debates among different spiritual traditions? For us, these debates highlight the very activities and energy of adult education and training. Moral choices infuse our practice as educators: judging learners, choosing what should be learned and how, and understanding human needs and our own response to these needs. Choosing a textbook or creating course assignments may seem commonplace, but every pedagogical activity is infused with moral and spiritual choice.

Consider a common goal for adult education and training — our call to help people live life to the full. Such a goal begs us to consider a number of important questions. What ethical right does an educator have to make spirituality explicit in developing communities of learners? What political and social dimensions of spirituality should we consider when working through issues that touch the soul of individual learners? What are the purpose and function of spirituality in building and leading learning communities? How are the practice, expression, and recognition of spirituality entwined with the concept of a learning community in which we are leaders? And, given the pluralistic communities of learners we all embrace, how can we understand truth and morality while appreciating various commitments to spirituality? Practicing as an adult educator or trainer today means knowing how to respond to these questions. But, even before that, it means having the insight to even consider these questions important. Adult educators or trainers can hardly even respond to these questions without being well-grounded in a particular spirituality.

Part of that grounding involves considering how to reconcile and make space for different spiritual beliefs and moralities in one's practice. We assume that, even in secular environments, domination by any single perspective is unacceptable. But, does this mean educators should simply assume all views are valid, and work toward tolerating, even making space for, all differences? We believe simplistic relativism as a doctrine for spirituality and morality is inadequate. Educators are not called to neutrality. Nor are they called to abdicate their responsibility to make moral choices, ensure learners' psychological safety, and advocate for equity. How then can educators find their way through spiritual paths to sort out the contradictions and distinguish the rich from the impoverished or manipulative?

We hope this chapter provides assistance. In it, we explore some common elements of spiritual discourse, showing continuums of differing beliefs within each element. These dimensions are combined into a theoretical framework we use to understand and categorize the various forms of spirituality mentioned throughout this book.

## DIMENSIONS FOR COMPARING DIFFERENT SPIRITUAL TRADITIONS

We have selected eight dimensions of spirituality for discussion and have organized these into the following sections:

1. Life and death (the meaning of life on earth or beyond)

2. Soul and self (the nature of spirit)

3. Cosmology (the nature of the spiritual universe, including higher powers)

4. Knowledge (the nature of truth)

5. The "Way" (the nature of the spiritual journey or search)

6. Focus (the purposes of spiritual seeking)

7. Practices of spirituality and the role of others

8. Responses (action and application arising from spiritual pursuits).

These were chosen using Taylor's (1996) model for comparing spiritualities as a starting point, then linking it with writers explicating spirituality from a broad, nonreligious base (such as Wilber, 1997).

## Life and Death (The Meaning of Life on Earth or Beyond)

How do we understand our lives? Part of the answer to this question depends on how we understand suffering, death, and whether we believe in a "life beyond." Some spiritual traditions focus on meeting worldly needs, enhancing, and empowering life. Other spiritual traditions focus on the transcendent. In these, life is meaningful to the extent that it affirms what matters beyond life. In such spiritual traditions, what matters isn't necessarily that which sustains life or causes it to flourish.

Taylor (1996) depicts spiritual traditions on a continuum. One end point is "transcendence"—renouncing ordinary life to seek those things beyond life. The opposite end point is "life-centeredness"—affirming life and dedicating spiritual search and activity to life's flourishing. As a way to compare spiritual traditions deeply, it is simplistic. However, placing different traditions along Taylor's continuum can help reveal their particular stances towards life. For example, Taylor situates most New Age spiritual traditions near the life-centeredness point in a "life-enhancement" stance. Towards the middle of the continuum lies what he calls a "complementary symbiosis" stance, reflecting an instrumentalizing of transcendence for the purpose of life-centeredness. An "agape/karuna" stance moves towards transcendence, but acknowledges that spirituality aimed beyond life to God's will ultimately brings one back to the enactment of God's will by the flourishing of human beings. Near the transcendence point is a "purity" stance. Here ordinary life is renounced as a goal of the spiritual journey.

Taylor (1996) suggests that most religions combine a concern for flourishing (life-centeredness) and renunciation (transcendence). This combination moves back and forth along the

continuum as cultures become preoccupied with certain values
and as historic shifts in social values occur. For example, there
are times in history when spiritual goodness is located in production, hard work, and the family. These become social icons
—as in the mythological "family values" of conservative Re-
publicans in the United States. In fact, they become almost em-
blems of a particular material form of life-centeredness—sort
of badges one earns by being prepared.

At other times in history, goodness has been connected to
a life-centeredness that spreads justice, benevolence, and equality,
relieving suffering and fostering prosperity. This stance echoes
Coady's (1939) integration of spiritual development with economic pragmatism. Thomas Moore (1994) has often rejected
the purist stance most evident in the monastic tradition currently enjoying a popular revival. He suggests its weakness is
that it abandons the human world of living and suffering to in-
dulge a lofty and esoteric path.

Educators working from spiritual bases, such as Palmer
(1983), tend to emphasize life-centeredness focused on relationships. Learning, writes Palmer, brings humans into engagement
and connection with each other and the world. This engagement
is inherently spiritual and transcendent; however, it is not a
breaking-out or removal from the world. Instead, it is a breaking-
in—the in-spiration of the Divine into material reality. This
understanding of transcendence rejects both the futuristic eschatology of the transcendent pole and the excessively material enactment of some spiritual traditions at the life-centeredness pole.
Its alternative, immanent eschatology, attempts to infuse reverence into daily human actions that seek complete communion
with the present moment. Thus, boundaries between the sacred
and secular dissolve.

Suffering and sacrifice represent interesting points of difference among spiritual beliefs about the nature of life. For some
faith traditions, suffering (including sin) is the state of the human condition. Suffering is to be accepted, dwelt in, learned
from, and possibly saved from. However, suffering is not necessarily a "fixed" state in our modernist sense of problem solving.
Self-sacrifice has been represented as a gift leading to grace

(Christianity), a discipline to tame desire (Buddhism), and a necessary door to losing the self and attaining enlightenment. However, other spiritual traditions treat suffering and sacrifice as obstacles to an enhanced, flourishing life. These traditions promote spiritual practices of self-sacrifice that help deliver us from these obstacles.

The idea of self-sacrifice is seen in most spiritual traditions. For example, Hinduism suggests that "Man, in truth, is himself a sacrifice" (cited in Wilson, 1991). Buddhism notes that "In accepting the true Dharma, may I abandon body, life, and property, and uphold the true Dharma." And, Christian self-sacrifice can be seen in a number of scripture passages. "Jesus told his disciples, 'If any man would come after me, let him deny himself and take up his cross and follow me. For whoever would save his life will lose it, and whoever loses his life from my sake will find it.' " And, "I appeal to you therefore, brethren, by the mercies of God, to present your bodies as a living sacrifice, holy and acceptable to God, which is your spiritual worship." Sikh literature notes that "With whatever Thou dost provide, am I content; No other door is there for me to knock. Nanak this supplication makes, May my life and body ever to Thee be dedicated!" Of course, self-sacrificial "suffering" may mean a variety of things. It could mean physical discomfort, guilt or fear, despair and sin, or a lack of truth, energy, joy, or any other desire. Each meaning provides a different slant on our sense of pain. Obviously, certain spiritual traditions place different values on physical or spiritual life, life here-and-now on earth or life beyond.

For example, some life-centered spiritual traditions either ignore or resist talk of death. Conversely, some ecological life-centered spiritual traditions view death and destruction as a natural part of the lifeworld and critical to transformation. The concept of kenosis in Buddhism, for example, means an "emptying out" of self, putting to death the self as a way to renounce the "grasping" ego. To help understand this concept, consider the ecological life of a forest. A forest thrives when it balances life, consumption, and death. Translated to human life, attempts to willfully preserve the life of one being above the natural order of all others can be viewed as misguided assertions of human control over the broader ecological cycles upon which life depends.

Some spiritual traditions acknowledge struggle as important parts of life, not to be avoided. Humans are expected to struggle with their mortality and failings. Questioning and doubting are not seen as a loss of faith, but accepted as part of the faith journey. Struggles with self, sin, desire, loss, and evil are represented, judged, explained, and assisted in spiritual traditions that address these deeper issues. For example, the Christian tradition sees confession and redemption as important pathways to a pure heart and communion with God. The problems of evil and the human struggle with evil surface in some spiritual traditions, but seem conveniently avoided in others. When any of these struggles are unnamed in a spirituality, the spiritual sojourner is deprived of strength. Sunny idealism and feel-good beliefs go only so far in explaining and working through life's complexity. They certainly do not mirror our life experiences.

> As perspective transformation theory so aptly points out, significant life experiences such as sickness, suffering, and death can sometimes lead to change in how adults see their world, and they can lead to a questioning of their assumptions and their life direction. Caryll Houselander, an early 20th-century spiritual writer, suffered a major physical illness of unknown causes when she was 8 years old. Miraculously, her mysterious illness disappeared when she received the Eucharist. This childhood experience influenced much of Houselander's subsequent writing and is seemingly connected to the mystical visions that she later experienced, as well as to her profound understanding of the indwelling of the divine in each of us. (Healey, 1989, p. 115)

## Soul and Self (The Nature of Spirit)

All spiritual traditions emanate from a fundamental understanding of soul. We believe it is helpful to examine some of these very different assumptions about the nature of self and its relation to spirit. Some spiritual traditions believe the self is fixed, autonomous, and coherent. Hillman (1996), for example, views soul as a uniqueness we are born with. Both a gift and a responsibility, soul demands to be lived, even though it is difficult to discern. Life's project is to understand one's soul and, in so doing, to find our "calling." Feminist writers argue that, for at least some people, self is relational, not autonomous. Self is revealed and enacted through connections, not through individual "self-actualization" (MacKeracher, 1996). The emphasis on "connection" profoundly extends through feminist spiritual traditions, which understand spirit to be interconnected and the purpose of spiritual journeys as the seeking of communion.

Still others believe humans have multiple, shifting selves which emerge in different situations and in the different stories we tell ourselves about our lives: "subjectivity without a centre of origin, caught in meanings, positioned in the language and narratives of the culture. . . . Meanings are always in play, and the self, caught up in this play, is an ever changing self" (Usher, Bryant, & Johnson, 1997, p. 103). Clark, an adult education theorist and former Roman Catholic nun, describes one's various selves as floating between one's biography, particular relationships, and language (Clark & Dirkx, 2000). Ken Wilber (1997) describes spirit as evolving through our various selves so that, through us, spirit sees and knows itself. The highest human state is that of divine witness.

Some spiritual traditions celebrate and glorify self, seeking to understand and pamper one's "authentic" self (Breathnach, 1995). However, in other spiritual pursuits self-surrender is a key dimension. For example, as noted earlier, Judeo-Christian traditions call followers to surrender the will, to give away one's life, and to find it in God and/or the communal. The emphasis of the Christian life is on servanthood and discipleship.

In Buddhist meditation, one learns to surrender one's desires and ego-self, as well as the search for absolute meaning itself (Buddhaghosa, 1976). Other spiritual writers also reflect this need. Oliver (1992) argues, working with the varied philosophies of Buber, Eckhart, Nishida Kitaro, and Orthodox

Christianity, that spiritual reality means understanding and dwelling in the "true" self, which is a "no-self." The self dissolves in the act of experiencing the world.

To know the true self—the no-self or the relational self—is to be one with the Divine. To be one means to be in communion and open to the indwelling of the spirit. The spiritual journey strives to relinquish the self's need to will its own purposes and determine its own expression. It accepts stillness and recognizes that the self is what it is now—being, not becoming.

> *Dorothy Day, cofounder with her colleague Peter Maurin, of the Catholic Worker Movement, led a life that was a study in paradoxes. She was a feminist, civil rights activist, proponent of communal living, single parent, and social justice advocate. Her deep sense of connectedness with the Spirit led her to start a religious, social and political movement that was dedicated to helping the poor. Dorothy understood profoundly the importance of knowing and loving herself and others. In her autobiography,* The Long Loneliness *(1952), she holds that we have all experienced loneliness in our lives. The cure is love, and love means relationships, and ultimately loving commitments.*

## Cosmology (The Nature of the Spiritual Universe, Including Higher Powers)

Attention to the notion of surrender must necessarily lead to new questions: To whom or what do the faithful surrender? If spirituality is a desire to transcend the self and commune with the divine, a yearning for redemption, a search for peace, and a willingness to surrender the self to a higher truth, what is accepted as the epistemic authority? For those who have surrendered rationality and ego to embrace more spiritual ways of knowing, how are truth claims constructed and adjudicated in the spiritual realm of mystery?

The simple answer is that people often simply believe in a higher power. Personal faith is often represented as a response to mystical spiritual experience, mediated through prayer. Slattery (1995) describes such meditation as "ruminating" silently on meaning and engaging the holy.

Theology, then, is the systematic hermeneutic study of the meaning of mystical experience. Personal spiritual journeys are grounded within carefully constructed theologies of belief that describe the sacred cosmos. Such a cosmos defines the nature of self and its relation to the divine, the relation of the present to eternity, the relation of the human world to the natural and supernatural, the grounds of moral reasoning, and prescriptions for behavior. All spiritual traditions share an interest in the nature of the sacred. How does the sacred "appear"? What are its demands? How is the sacred infused into daily life? How can it be glimpsed? Can it be recovered? Spiritual time is also an important dimension of the cosmos. What is eternity? What is tradition? What is history, and how important is it? What does it mean to live within "the present moment"? Which of the many concepts of time should preoccupy our interests?

An important dimension of spirituality is understanding how energy and power flow through the spiritual universe. Different spiritual traditions represent the source and circulation of energy differently. The presence of a higher power for some is monotheistic (one God), for others polytheistic (many gods), and for others pantheistic (god in all things). Some traditions do not believe in a theistic authority. Some view energy as human empowerment or community-based; some view it as ecological. Creation-centered theology (whose proponents include Thomas Berry and Matthew Fox) emphasizes intimacy between the human and natural worlds, and perceives all living as a communion of subjects rather than a collection of objects.

*Twelfth-century German mystic, poet, and musician Hildegard of Bingen (1987) is a source of inspiration for many today, in part because she had the insight to see the divine essence present in all things: "[God is speaking:] I, the highest and fiery power, have kindled every spark of life . . . I, the fiery life of divine essence, am aflame beyond the beauty of the meadows, I gleam in the waters, and I burn*

*in the sun, moon, and stars. With every breeze, as with in-
visible life that contains everything, I awaken everything to
life. The air lives by turning green and being in bloom. The
waters flow as if they were alive. The sun lives in its light,
and the moon is enkindled, after its disappearance, once
again by the light of the sun so that the moon is again re-
vived. . . . And thus I remain hidden in every kind of reality
as a fiery power. Everything burns because of me in such a
way as our breath constantly moves us, like the wind-tossed
flame in a fire." (pp. 8, 10)*

Whenever humans ask questions about a higher power in
the spiritual universe, the issue and nature of our relationships
with that higher power burst forth. Some spiritual traditions
approach this relationship as the ultimate goal; some, as the
starting point. From this point they then address human goals—
ranging from fulfillment of worldly desires to attainment of
otherworldly enlightenment. Different spiritual traditions also
understand the relationship between humans and a higher
power differently. For some, it is highly personal; for others, it
is mainly community-centered. Sometimes a spiritual leader
mediates relationships. And, obviously, relationships are approached in a variety of ways—sometimes through worship,
ritual, prayer, sacrifice, and/or action. Some people run from
God in fear; others seek to embrace God in celebration.

Finally, spiritual traditions can be distinguished by the relation they see between human will and God's will. Some describe their purpose as seeking greater control over their lives
through spiritual growth. Others work from a paradigm of
seeking surrender to the will or dynamics of a power in the universe greater than the individual human.

## Knowledge (The Nature of Truth)

Discussing the nature of knowledge is a broad-ranging dialogue that extends far beyond the purpose of this chapter. In
spiritual terms, differences in understanding what knowledge is

and what counts as knowledge can be distinguished along three dimensions: (1) the possibility of truth or truths; (2) the presence of a higher power; and (3) the role of the human seeker for truth.

Some spiritual traditions rest on a foundation of absolute truth. While these traditions are often labeled "fundamentalist," there are varying degrees of fundamentalism. We define fundamentalism as a strong belief in a particular doctrine. Implicitly, we also define fundamentalism as generally intolerant of contradicting beliefs.

Other spiritual traditions accept multiple truths, although there are degrees of genuine acceptance of different beliefs. Sometimes the boundaries or the possibility of evolution among beliefs are fluid, accepting one thing and rejecting another as circumstances seem to dictate. For example, Wilber (1997) advocates "perspectivism" and the integration of different points of view to better detect the contours of human experience. But he does not believe in simple, "anything goes" relativism. Instead, he advocates a thoughtful commitment to gaining a depth of perspective, by engaging in spiritual perspectives different from our own. Wilber suggests that, instead of asking which approach is right and which is wrong, we assume each approach contains partial truth. Then we try to figure out how to integrate these partial truths. Our purpose should focus on how to use truth, not how to pick one truth and throw away another.

God is, in some spiritual traditions, all-knowing, all-seeing, and completely trustworthy as the center of truth. Humans, by contrast, are not gods because the best they can do is to attain partial truth in this life. In other faith traditions, deities are powerful but partially knowing characters. In these traditions, humans need to understand and mediate their messages. For all theistic traditions (where knowledge is linked to a "higher power"), theistic authority is sometimes revealed through divine or supernatural revelation and prophetic message. For some traditions, knowledge is more human-centered or nature-centered than god-centered. In different spiritual communities, personal mystical knowing may be questioned and regulated through disciplines, doctrine, or spiritual practices and study.

Spiritual humans share the desire to seek truth. But, as always, there is a variety of paradigms of truth. All different spiritual truths, however, contain their own version of wisdom and enlightenment. They also encourage faith in something and the acceptance of some answers to the mystery of life and death as opposed to other answers. Sometimes knowledge is seen as the "key" to spiritual growth; sometimes it is seen as a dangerous door to a loss of innocence—the fruit of the tree of knowledge of good and evil. Some spiritual traditions insist on long study; others celebrate intuition and simplicity. Some even seem to reject spiritual knowledge, emphasizing emotional release and ecstatic communion above thought and rationality.

Finally, the adherents of spiritual traditions must view their lives in the present through the lens of spiritual tradition. This is not always easy. Some spiritual traditions struggle with modern life. Their traditional dogma or doctrine seems to collide with today's tempo of living. Things just don't seem to fit well. New converts are hard to find and those who do convert often want quicker answers than the spiritual tradition can give. Modern Jewish scholars describe the problem with the newly popularized Kabballah faith by referring to a traditional light/fire phenomenon in spirituality. The truth we long for cannot be controlled, hurried, or "applied," and it often bites (Wiltz, 1997). But, even here, the experiences of a Jewish scholar and humans who live and work in the everyday world differ. The answers that console one often do not console the other.

## The "Way" (The Nature of the Spiritual Journey or Search)

Examining a broad range of spiritual traditions, educator Slattery (1995) suggests that "the spiritual" is the "self in dialogue with eternal communal wisdom" (p. 81), searching for both personal and universal peace. The human spirit senses a holy center to life where all things are interconnected, and seeks to recover and nurture it. Through spiritual activities, infused with a deliberate reaching inwards and outwards, the individual human spirit approaches union with the cosmos as a complex, integrated entity and with the mystery of eternity. Slattery's (1995) sense of a human journey towards a mysterious union highlights our own definition of "spirituality." We believe the spiritual domain includes, among other things, a person's struggles to understand self, soul, and purpose; to develop the "spirit" or "higher consciousness"; to conceptualize the problem of evil and the definition of good; to specify values and choose actions for "right" living; and to seek communion with that mysterious realm sometimes described as interconnectedness, Spirit, the divine, holiness, or the cosmos.

However, the nature of this journey varies among spiritual traditions according to several dimensions. We have alluded to some of these in previous sections. First, spirituality has a dimension of time—be it a lifetime, a quick healing, or a time beyond life. Perhaps this meaning of time reaches through several human lives or into a heavenly afterlife. Second, spirituality questions the extent of personal freedom to control and make choices along this journey. This freedom contrasts to faith or surrender to other energies and dynamics. A related third point questions the place of spirituality in one's life. Is the spiritual journey seen as simply one dimension of life, coexisting with but supporting intellectual life, marital life, career, and creativity? Or are other parts of life subordinate to the spiritual life? This dimension is closely connected to Taylor's (1996) continuum, which distinguishes between an essential focus on life-centeredness or on transcendence. Fourth, spirituality has a dimension of community. Is the spiritual journey seen as a solitary sojourn or a connective, communal journey? Fifth, spirituality includes a dimension of action. Is one's spirituality more meditative or action-oriented? Sixth, spirituality includes a dimension of emotion. What is the emotional content of the journey? How are peak experiences understood, and what role do they play? Conversely, what is the role of negativity, questioning, and doubting on the journey in contrast to an emphasis on the positive: joy, healing, peace, and happiness? Is the journey a more cerebral, intellectual truth-seeking? Does it understand emotions as distractive or ego-grasping? Seventh, spirituality always includes a destination. How is the outcome of a spiritual journey portrayed?

Some spiritual traditions represent the spiritual journey in terms of growth, in a Western "development/improvement" paradigm. Fowler (1981), for example, identifies six progressive stages of spiritual growth (see Chapter 5). But Fowler's approach contrasts with spiritual traditions that seek to accept and dwell in mystery. These traditions accept, rather than try to "fix" or improve humans—as if the spiritual journey were just another technique of self-help (Moore, 1994). Most depictions of the spiritual journey include a concern for discernment and desire to distinguish the "true" path from "false" ones. Sometimes this concern asks: How do we remain open to the spirit stirring within us, without distraction from world-lusts and ego-desires? As Egan (1996) writes, "We are always headed somewhere, but which wind is in our sails?" (p. 8).

> *A classic of Russian spiritual literature is the anonymous publication* The Pilgrim Continues His Way *(1986). This is the story of a pilgrim who travels to the holy places of Russia and learns from people along the way. On one occasion, in a town near Kiev, the pilgrim discusses prayer with a priest. The priest provides the pilgrim with notes that instruct him in how he must live out his journey: The priest says, "[you] must arouse in your soul a thirst and a longing —or, as some call it 'wonder' which brings you an insatiable desire to know things more closely and more fully, to go deeper into their nature." (p. 29)*

## Focus (The Purposes of Spiritual Seeking)

Bass (1998), a professor of religious studies at Rhodes College, wrote a reaction to an article in *Self Magazine* suggesting that seekers of inner solace might choose a little Zen, a little Christianity, a little nature worship, and so on. Disgusted by fast food approaches to spirituality, Bass presented the spiritual journey of most faiths as longer but more satisfying, with two

interwoven parts—the inner self and the outer transcendent. She
notes the weakness of spiritual traditions that concentrate only
on the inner journey of healing, seeking personal peace, questioning, and exploring the self in relation to mysteries greater
than the self.

Those writing about spirituality often use the inner-outer
dialectic. Wilber (1997), for example, defines spirituality as an
inward path of evolving consciousness and spirit. But, other
spiritual traditions emphasize an outward journey, reaching towards others in interconnectedness and faith expressed in actions of servanthood. Mack (1992) emphasizes an outward perspective, describing the spiritual journey as humans engaging
the world deeply, integrating spiritual perspectives in gritty
everyday material reality. For Mack, spirituality is closely linked
with working out everyday actions of morals, relationships, and
values.

Bass (1998), however, maintains that inner and outer journeys are simultaneous and must be interwoven. Principe (1997)
explains spirituality as a dual movement, inward and outward,
that ultimately seeks "life in the Spirit" (p. 112). He writes
about Spirit as a divine holiness moving through and connecting
the world, time, and individual souls. Dialogues such as these
highlight the importance of purpose as a distinguishing dimension of spiritual traditions. Individuals pursue spiritual journeys
for motives that range from self-focused (such as seeking redemption, repentance, rebirth) and self-serving (becoming more
creative, happy, healthy) to more other-directed (caring and connecting to others and to create community).

The purposes of spiritual journeys also range from more
worldly to other-worldly, and from more inquiry oriented to
more action oriented. Action oriented spiritual traditions, such
as the liberation theologies of social justice, are described later
in this chapter. The personal expansion of one's creative capacity
is sometimes a purpose of spirituality. Degler's (1996) book *The
Fiery Muse: Creativity and the Spiritual Quest* outlines the connection between creative genius and spiritual experience. Degler
notes that the goal of Eastern yogic practices (shakit, kundalini,

prana) is to access inner energy to achieve an extreme state of awakening which infuses the human brain with power, light, and bursts of intense creativity. But, where some spiritual traditions seek truth and higher consciousness, other writers such as Moore (1994) criticize "the project of an enlightened self" as being modernist and narcissistic.

The ideas of purpose and motive within spiritual pursuits are continually troubled by the problem of desire. Why are we drawn to this or that spirituality, this or that vocation, this or that drive to possess? Some spiritual traditions represent this problem as discerning our "true" desire, putting to death the misleading destructive desires of our grasping life to awaken to "true" life.

MacPherson (1996), for example, describes Tantric Buddhism as an education of desire, transcending dualisms of right and wrong and a cult of consumption and production to find a path of moderation. For others, desire for greater wisdom, wealth, and success is celebrated as the fuel and reward of spiritual endeavor. Finally, some people seem blissfully untroubled by motive.

## Practices of Spirituality and the Role of Others

Slattery (1995) writes that the spiritual seeks union with the mystery of eternity through practices such as meditation, ecclesiastic and daily ritual, divine revelation, theological discipline, service to others, participation in community, human relationships, work, and learning. Most spiritual traditions incorporate community rituals as a way to create sacred spaces together, as well as to provide private spaces where personal meditation and prayer allow the spirit to flourish. Later, in Chapter 3, we will offer some variations on these practices as exercises in strengthening and exploring one's own spirituality. Some spiritual practices are equated to a discipline with routine, rules, and even sacrifice. Some doctrines, for example, call followers to love and compassion in a life of reverent relationships.

These spiritual journeys are regulated through disciplines of responsibility, duty, service, and continuous testing of spiritual
understandings through rigorous discernment.

Mindfulness is a discipline of both Celtic spiritual traditions (De Waal, 1997) and Buddhism. It invokes wide-awake attention to and engagement with all parts of one's being to each
full moment (MacPherson, 1996). The discipline of Buddhist
meditation seeks to develop the ability to be present with one's
mind in the experiences of everyday life (Silandanda, 1990). The
strict discipline of some spiritual traditions stands in contrast to
spiritual traditions that eschew regulation of any kind or that
focus only on spontaneous, ad hoc practices.

> *The art and practice of mindfulness have been well
> developed in the writing of Vietnamese Buddhist monk,
> Thich Nach Hahn (1990). Hahn tells the story of being in
> Montreal and seeing the French phrase "je me souviens" (I
> will remember) on the license plates of cars. He suggested
> to his friend that every time he sees those words (often, if
> he spent any time in traffic) he should remember to "breathe
> and smile." Needless to say riding in a car in Montreal traf-
> fic will never be the same.*

The role of others in spiritual pursuits ranges from peers
joined in supportive community (brothers and sisters) to priests,
prophets, and spiritual directors acting as visionaries, leaders,
and facilitators of the journey. The idea of soul friends describes a rich spiritual relationship that we discuss in the next
chapter. But what about the educator?

Teaching and learning, Palmer (1983) suggests, are ancient
communal acts. They can be renewed through any practice
of spiritual wisdom that welcomes inquiry and does not fear
searching. Others also see the educator as guiding inquiry. Purpel (1989) promotes the infusion of the sacred into education,
calling teachers to be prophets in a learning process that seeks
ultimate meaning. Some educators in the tradition of Freire
hear the educator's call as enabling spiritual transformation.
MacPherson (1996), applying Tantric Buddhism to adult educa-

tion, suggests a radical redefinition of the educator as a "healer, a therapist, and an essential catalyst of personal, social, and environmental transformation" (p. 468).

## Responses (Action and Application Arising from Spiritual Pursuits)

From a spiritual perspective, the question of the educator's role is partly a question of right response. How, for example, can action be inspired by a spiritual pursuit? This question is answered differently in various spiritual traditions. Transformation is only one correct answer. This section outlines some key dimensions of difference among the others.

Correct response depends on one's purpose for pursuing spirituality. In a life-centered spiritual orientation, the purpose of expanding one's potential (creativity, vocation) might provoke responses such as Cameron's (1992) exercises to become more artistic. She discusses writing morning pages to overcome blocks, giving oneself permission to "let go" and widen creative horizons. This exercise in described in Chapter 3. Purposes such as seeking personal therapy, repentance, "healing," and peace of mind might inspire prayer, spiritual retreats and reflective dialogue, or transformative action to change one's life. Purposes of seeking enlightenment for self-knowledge, clearer vocation, deeper meaning of life, or an exploration of different levels of consciousness may be manifested in study and other learning pursuits.

Spirituality is often expressed as a human yearning for redemption. Some people are desperate for forgiveness and salvation. They turn to spirituality to free them from fear, anxiety, and pain. Some spiritualists promise that rest and salvation can be found only in a turning to God—a transpersonal, mystical experience of total reality bridging the now and the human with the divine. Here, according to Jager (1995), all appears complete and perfect.

Mack (1992) suggests that spiritual response is a meaningful connection with others to escape the alienating power and regulation of modern society's urges to dominate, acquire, possess, and control. The spiritual experience, explains Mack, is one of harmony, peace, and living interconnectedly with all life. The spiritual impulse thus renounces possessions and materiality and embraces a fluid existence of seeking meaningfulness and reverent relationships.

Adult educators and trainers are often compelled by their own spiritual desires to serve. But, what constitutes service is hardly agreed upon. Responding to the spiritual need to serve in some spiritual traditions is broad-based, spreading far afield for social transformation (as in liberation theologies). In some evangelistic traditions, it is based upon the conversion of others. Some spiritual traditions concentrate on accepting what is and liberating oneself within this truth, as in the Benedictine way to find direction and humility in community, seeking joy where one is at present (De Waal, 1984).

In organizational management literature, Greenleaf (1998) has written about "servant leadership" as a moral undertaking. Block (1993) uses the term *stewardship* to represent a way of choosing service over self-interest. Service may be enacted in building or transforming communities, cultivating sacred environments towards a "spirit-filled" world, or simply attending with love to another person. In some spiritual traditions, service places emphasis more on charity; in others, more on justice.

The idea of living with pain is universal in spiritual traditions. To touch pain is to awaken to injustice. Pain links humans to each other for pain is schooling in compassion (Fox, 1983). Compassion for all life forms breaks down boundaries of identity, and consequently abandons systems of power and cravings for possession predicated on difference. From the deep recesses of private pain, compassion embraces the powerless and exploited as well as the powerful and prosperous, who together share weariness and drained hope. In such a spiritual view, justice means more than rational, abstract rules of law. Instead, justice means a passionate caring that, as Gandhi suggested, loves people into transformation. This spiritual response echoes the work of theology-trained adult educator Myles Horton, who celebrated common human experience to liberate human empowerment in civil rights struggles in the southern United States.

Liberation theology and emancipatory pedagogy share the long tradition of uniting spiritual search with critical thinking and social action. Recently, curriculum theorists such as Slattery (1995) and theologians such as Griffin (1988) have begun to articulate a common vision that links spirituality with education as a process of personal and civic transformation. Slattery contends that religion and education are inseparable. He outlines a constructive, postmodern vision which threads "ethical and ecumenical integration of spirituality and theology into the very fabric of education" (p. 68).

Slattery's (1995) vision presents three ways learning communities might integrate educational processes with spirituality:

1. An emphasis on community cooperation rather than corporate competition promotes "a search for wisdom through theological experiences, that creates cooperative and ecologically sustainable learning environments, and that commits to reverent, democratic, and just community models of schooling" (p. 94).

2. A holistic process perspective (rather than reductionism) connects the past and present to the eternal.

3. A multilayered interdisciplinary curriculum integrates spirituality and theology into all aspects of the educational process.

In many spiritual traditions, work has long been acknowledged as a reflection of human creativity, constituting human dignity and sustaining human community. Gutierrez (1968), a liberation theologian, believes that "work as a humanizing element normally tends through this transformation of nature to construct a society that is more just and worthy of human beings. Every offense, every humiliation, every alienation of human labor is an obstacle to the work of salvation" (p. 2). The three emphases on community cooperation, holistic learning, and the integration of education with the spiritual can be consolidated into a new vision of the workplace that merges learning and work.

However, for adult educators and trainers, a fundamental question remains. Is the corporation, with its particular interests, a legitimate site for overt integration of learning processes with spirituality? The problem of finding a defensible line between the individual and the legitimate prerogative of the secular educational institution becomes slippery when purposes such as developing "right" hearts and spirits are declared. We encourage a secular organization that is dedicated to creating a compassionate life-giving environment, one that is concerned with helping people find fulfillment and personal meaning in their learning and living, and one that tries to nurture connectedness and caring. When considering actions and applications of spirituality in education, the compelling questions remain, as always, the same:

1. What is the real intent of educational initiatives which integrate or emphasize on spirituality?

2. Who benefits, and how?

3. What conception of need drives the initiative, according to whose perception, and by whose authority?

4. Whose beliefs, needs, or identities are potentially excluded or eroded?

5. What other potential consequences can be anticipated, to individuals and to the collective? How are these justified as desirable?

Such motivation should be evident in an organization's fundamental commitment to the work-life-learning balance of its people. Emphasis might be less on programs for individuals' spiritual training and more on flexible hours, support for employees' volunteer work outside the company, child-care and elder-care support, compassionate response to people's stress, challenge of exclusive practices, exercise of social responsibility

in the wider community, and clear evidence that the organization questions and practices a consistent and thoughtful system
of ethics in all areas of its activity. Such responses to the spiritual
impulse stir the entire organization in humility and authentic
search for justice, towards a vision that Griffin (1988) articu-
lates as public life grounded in a postmodern theology, "a re-
enchantment of the cosmos and a better intuition of its " 'Holy
Centre' " (p. 52).

> *Mindfulness and spirituality may be fostered by spiri-
> tuality but they are surely not limited by place—all loca-
> tions have spiritual possibilities. An Egyptian desert mo-
> nastic Amma Syncletica observed: "It is possible to be
> solitary in one's mind while living in a crowd, and it is pos-
> sible for one who is solitary to live in the crowd of his own
> thoughts." (Ward, 1975, p. 196)*

## SUMMARY

In this chapter we have presented eight dimensions we believe are important in different spiritual traditions. We have then
generally discussed some of the essential differences within these
dimensions. The eight dimensions of life and death, soul and
self, cosmology, knowledge, the "Way," focus, practice and others' role, and responses are all interrelated. Different spiritual
traditions represent these eight dimensions in different and particular ways of seeing, believing, and acting in the world.

We believe it is crucial that educators examine these dimensions thoughtfully and evaluate carefully the wild explosion of
spiritual traditions clamoring for disciples today. We need to discern the motives and centers of different spiritual traditions, as
well as our own motives and the source of our attraction to
them.

Are we simply seeking a feel-good self-affirmation? Are
we seeking to escape uncertainty and rapid change through
simple answers? Are we fleeing responsibility for making tough

choices by seeking ready-made systems of values or gurus creating pathways for living? Do we seek to hide from life's pain in rosy panaceas—ignoring darker purposes moving underneath some spiritual promises?

Only by examining the interplay of light and darkness in both the public society and the private corners of one's heart can one discern the integrity of various spiritual traditions. As we have suggested, the process of discernment moves beyond intellectual reductionism and categorizing. Discernment means identifying the inner will to possess and control, and the artificial construction of a self driven by fear and a need for self-affirmation (Del Prete, 1990, p. 36). In the realm of spiritual experience, it may be difficult to distinguish between the inner stirring of truth, whether it be divine authority or awareness of the communal and eternal, and the consumptive lusts and compulsions of our own grasping egos.

Certainly we need to be critical and wary of the agendas, promises, interests, and portrayal of humans in the world embedded in any sense of spirituality. Still, as important as critical thinking is, rational approaches must be balanced with intuitive, spiritual listening. Discernment calls for a stilling of the rambling conscious mind and a deeper awakening to the moment, a learning to be being fully present to the sacred. Egan (1996) also suggests listening to the testimonies of the mystics and the voices of women, the poor, the marginalized, and the excluded. Most of all, he suggests that "we must struggle against our inordinate attachment to worldly values and partial truths and zones of comfort . . . it is love that most reveals the divine presence—a joyful, generous, extravagant, and self-transcending love" (p. 9).

---

## STARTING POINTS FOR FURTHER REFLECTION

To choose among the voices and expressions of spirituality, where, how, and to whom should we listen? One place adult educators or trainers might start is to examine their own biographies. Think about the following questions:

1. For many of us it is important to acknowledge and perhaps reconcile the influence of our religious upbringing on our current spiritual preferences and avoidances. What is the most significant spiritual experience from your childhood? Close your eyes and bring that experience to mind. Who was there? What you were thinking? Feeling? Hoping? Experiencing?

2. What messages about religion and spirituality did you receive in your home? How have you carried these messages into your adult life? How do they influence your current work?

# CHAPTER 3

## Developing Our Spirituality

Everyone understands spirituality as a part of popular culture, but many people wonder how spirituality can be integrated into their everyday lives or have meaning outside religious structures or practices. While reading this chapter, we encourage adult educators and trainers to think about how they might personally integrate spirituality into their own lives and work. We will, especially, invite you to consider some specific practices that various spiritual travelers have offered. These include adopting a spiritual perspective, bodywork, meditation and contemplation, reflective reading, journal writing, participating in rituals, and cultivating soul friends. We assume that those who read this book are interested in their own spirituality and are consciously exploring either disciplines and practices that fit best with their own lives. These ways and means can be engaged lightly or deeply, as moments of solace or as openings to a sacred unknown. For many sojourners they represent a lifelong commitment to being whole, living life to the fullest, and being creative about how to live.

### CONFRONTING OUR FEARS

Adult educators and trainers can incorporate a spiritual dimension into their teaching in a number of different ways. These include honoring spiritual questions from learners, challenging learners to consider how particular topics affect their spirituality, and supporting dialogue about crucial life issues such as death and illness. However, educators and trainers should face head-on certain fears we and our learners may have about how spirituality intersects with our vocation. If we cannot discuss these concerns in depth, learners may never attempt to make their own interconnections, despite how much they may want to. These fears include the accusation that we as "spiritual" teachers hope to proselytize learners, the danger that we will be considered anti-intellectual or nonrigorous by learners, and the scorn of colleagues who may label us as biased, fundamentalist, "way out there," or simply unprofessional.

We may be afraid our conversation will seem out of place, that somehow we are crossing a line that separates the personal from the professional. We may also be afraid, in some strange way, that others will come to know our vulnerabilities and discover that we have a deep thirst to know the natural world, each other, and ourselves better. In today's academic climate of critique and deconstruction, those who ascribe to one particular belief system may fear accusation of intellectual narrowness and intolerance.

However, we find it difficult to be progressive and courageous about supporting learners and challenging dominant norms without holding some "grand narrative." That is, we believe our vocation calls us to work towards some justifiable, worthwhile goal. We as adult educators and trainers interested in integrating a spiritual aspect into our practice need to spend time thinking about what spirituality means to us, personally. We need to confront the reality that our work may become suspect and our work environments critiqued because we are as interested in spirituality on Monday as on Saturday or Sunday.

It is one thing to practice our own spiritual disciplines and quite another to bring a spiritual theme to our educational and training practice. As Zinn (1997) has pointed out, there are both fears and definite barriers to integrating spirituality into adult education and training. Talking about spirituality in the classroom is intimidating for many adult educators and trainers. First, we may fear we have trodden where only ministers, shamans, gurus, and rabbis ought to go. Yet, we also believe deep inside that to ignore spirituality in our relationships and in our teaching and learning is to hide an important part of who we are. If we were successful in keeping our spirituality hidden, we would hide from others the fact that our relationships comprise a meaning-making function. We would also be suggesting, by our actions, that spirituality can be denied, when in fact we know it cannot.

One of the greatest fears learners may encounter is the fear of moving away from their easiest, most comfortable place of living. We may talk a good game, but when it comes to actually expanding our capacities and our ways of thinking, we tend to balk. Spiritual writer Williamson (1993) says that our greatest fear is not of our weakness, but of our strength. Most of us are afraid to be as great as we really are, even though we are meant to radiate the greatness of the Divine that is within us. Para-doxically, as we let our light shine, we invite others to let theirs shine as well (pp. 188–189). Fear of our ability and our success cannot be allowed to scare and intimidate us. By taking the time to think about this fear and to minimize its presence in our own lives and work, we can move ahead. It is an exciting challenge.

## SPIRITUAL PERSPECTIVE

Working on our spiritual lives is complex. It begins first by examining our spiritual perspective, our outlook on work, our personal life, our way of being in the world, and our belief in the purpose in life. It is a "big-picture" worldview that gives our lives coherence, connects professional and personal, and helps us see the meaning in life and work. When we question our pur-pose, we must ask: What are we about as adult educators and trainers? What is our place in this field? What should our work accomplish or move towards? What gives our work meaning? Our examination of purpose moves us far beyond naming iso-lated practices and techniques we can "use" to make us spiritual. Examining our purpose helps us both develop a vision and come to understand our spiritual place in the world.

Collins (1991) has astutely argued that adult education is, or ought to be, about more than techniques or tricks of practice. Similarly, reducing spirituality to the level of instructional gimmicks is antithetical to the spirit of adult education and training. Collins calls us back to adult education and training as "vocation" that "entails firm commitment to the performance of worthwhile activities that are not merely calculated to advance personal career aspirations or fulfil minimum job expectations" (p. 42). Spirituality echoes Collins's themes of vocation. As adult educators and trainers live their lives, they live their vocation. They deliberately make "careful, self-conscious reflections about one's work—an intellectual commitment" (Collins, 1991, p. 42). The vocation of adult education and training entails a total spiritual commitment to the common good and constant self-examination of our spiritual purpose or our reason for being. Spirituality is, as Auden (1940) said of poetry, "a way of happening" and a way of understanding and living our vocation in the world.

Of the many spiritual writers who have explored the notion of vocation as a spiritual journey, two of the more prolific are Evelyn and James Whitehead (1995). Like Collins (1991), the Whiteheads are unafraid to amplify the word *vocation* for its rich, multidimensional meanings. And like Collins, the Whiteheads describe vocation as knowing "our lives are more than accidental, that we are 'for something'" (p. 14).

When we think of our work as a vocation, it helps us understand that our lives have direction, purpose, and meaning. This understanding influences how we live in the world and how our own lifelong adult education and training journey unfolds. According to the Whiteheads (1995), vocation "has taken root through the influence of loved ones, the witness of communities, the force of cherished ideals" (p. 14).

Rather than thinking of adult education or training as a job we perform, when we consider it a vocation, we orient ourselves to our relationships, our work, our selves, and the earth. For some, vocation becomes a journey. This journey unfolds in a variety of ways and is lived out as we mature in relationships with ourselves, others, the natural world, and often with a higher power. For others, the journey metaphor may seem too linear and focused on moving forward—the old notion of Western progress. Other metaphors may reflect spirituality as the gentle oscillations of breath or a wave, as expanding space, or as burrowing-down. When the vocation of adult education and training is seen as a spiritual journey, we place emphasis more on the process than on the destination itself. The poet Kavafy (1989) in his poem "Ithaca" tells us to keep the end in view—in his case, the mythical isle Ithaca—but not to rush the trip since the trip itself is the gift (pp. 6, 22–23).

The Whiteheads (1995) have further developed the journey metaphor. They describe vocation as play, not drudgery. Rather than portraying work and life as separate spheres—with work as joyless "drudgery" or toil—they offer the image of play to describe vocation. This notion enhances the sense of joy and delight they believe should be part of one's vocation. Their vision of vocation is imbued with joy. It constantly interplays and blurs the divisions between light and dark, seriousness and lightness, joy and sorrow. To them, vocation encompasses emotion and body, joy and sweetness, life and fun.

The Whiteheads also suggest a variety of ways to view our vocation in the world, each directly and intricately connected to how we think the world is constructed or created and what we consider our place in it. Frequently, we live out our understanding of vocation without ever naming it explicitly. Yet, the way we live reflects deep-rooted assumptions we hold about the world and our relationship to it.

To develop their point, the Whiteheads delineate three ways to view creation, the setting in which we live out a vocation, and how we develop an understanding of our vocation. First, we may view creation as something we *inhabit*. In this worldview, a divine being has given us a static world. Our response is to live out a plan for our lives, or our vocation, in a preordained universe created by a mysterious creator who controls all and who asks only that we live here. As adult educators and trainers, our role is stable and unchanging. For adult educators and trainers, this view of vocation calls for a strict observance and following of orders and rules. Adult educators and trainers may make choices, but their main job is to preserve tradition.

The Whiteheads' second framework proposes that creation

is something worked by humans. In this worldview, a divine being created the universe and allowed humans to finish it. Humans, then, continue the work of creation. In this industrial model, vocation demands that we continue or finish this divinely inspired work in the cosmos. As humans, we are given labor and pleasure; but, ultimately our capacity to think, to imagine, and to act is limited. Adult educators and trainers with this worldview see themselves as industrial workers who must plug away, but who cannot change radically what has been inherited.

The Whiteheads' third framework views creation as something that is *played*. This framework implies that humans delight in creation, and that we create and improvise the events of our lives as we go. As adults, we are acting out our lives with a certain air of playfulness and enjoyment. Vocation is not doing what we are told, but rather it is inventing, creating, and making meaning in our lives.

This playing framework is the view of spirituality and vocation put forward in this book. Vocation is the playing out of creation through companionship and delight. We agree with the Whiteheads' desire to rescue the word *play* from the obvious connotations of frivolity. According to them, "It is rather with companionship and delight that creation is played" (p. 25). The scenes and the acts of life are not all scripted. Adult educators and trainers have a playful, creative role in their own and others' vocational process.

To live in creation is to play. Using the word *play* suggests to us that we all need to take breaks from our work—to rest, as the Bible so often suggests. Too often we view play as wasteful and nonproductive, when in fact it has many positive dimensions, beginning with the suggestion that it adds enthusiasm to learning. Of course, play has an immediate connection with Mark Twain's note that "work consists of what one has to do, and play of what one wants to do."

The Whiteheads note that a playful view of creation, and ultimately vocation, "demands that we be energetic and assertive players, willing to contest, able to push against" (p. 28) all that

constrains us. This views adult education and training as creative, robust and lively, and replete with successes and failures—
grappling constantly with the unknown and that which cannot
be known. In short, it is a way of thinking about life and work
and education that values humans as full, active change agents
with unlimited possibilities and obstacles. And it views the obstacles themselves as possibilities in the waiting room.

> *The re-creational aspect of play is well illustrated by
> the lives of the fourth- and-fifth century monks in the Egyp-
> tian desert. These monks were among the earliest examples
> of spirituality in the Christian East. Their stories, primarily
> told in short, pithy sayings, are full of instruction about
> everyday spirituality—for them, a balance of creation and
> re-creation. St. Anthony is greeted by a busy hunter. The
> hunter is shocked that St. Anthony is relaxing outside his
> hut instead of being busy "doing God's work." So St. An-
> thony instructs the hunter to repeatedly shoot his arrow.
> Somewhat puzzled, the hunter does so. Finally he stops.
> "Sir," he protests, "My bow is about to break." St. Anthony
> replies, "So it is with the monk. If we push ourselves be-
> yond measure we will break; it is right from time to time
> to relax our efforts." (Ward, 1975, p. 3)*

The importance of the notion of play in adult education
and training has been developed by Lanie Melamed (1987), who
interviewed nine women over 40 who said they learned best
through play. Melamed's interest in conducting the study origi-
nated from her own positive experiences of learning while playing. She observed that "the quality of my work improves when
I can play at things, when I have time to try alternatives, when
I can see, touch, laugh, and be physically involved in the learning
process" (p. 14). Spurred by curiosity whether her experiences
were unique, she interviewed participants to further understand
their experiences. She found that, for these women, play was not
just a pleasurable activity—it was a way of living and learning
in the world. Melamed's study led her to believe that play melds
the imagination and instinct with politics and reconstruction.

Playful learning is relational and involves cooperation with others. It is experiential, integrating the physical, emotional, social, cognitive, and spiritual. It is metaphoric, relying on rapid intuitive connections and leaps. And, it helps empower the transformation of others and ourselves.

This understanding of vocation and of spirituality challenges us as adult educators and trainers to ask some very basic questions. What are the roots of our own vocation? What drives our work? What are our assumptions about our vocation? Do we bring a sense of play as a creative and active force, where humans are active agents who take initiative, care for self and others, and are creative in the world? Do we have a sense that the final act in our vocational story is not yet written? If not, what might that act be?

A playful notion of vocation, when applied to the work of adult education and training, allows practitioners to be flexible in what they do and why they do it. It also allows us room for both success and failure and, perhaps more importantly, it allows us to redefine the concepts of success and failure. Play is hardly new to adult education or training (Melamed, 1987). Play suggests a world that allows risk taking, testing of limits, and flexibility. Play is robust and strong; it allows turbulence and even chaos, and provides opportunities to learn that all our hopes and dreams do not, cannot, will not come to fruition. To view one's vocation as play also leaves room for failure in our lives and work. It allows us to dream, but reminds us that the dreams we have for both our vocation and ourselves may remain unfulfilled. It also allows us ways to express the disappointment we feel when our dreams are not realized (Levinson et al., 1978).

The Whiteheads (1995) note that the strength of a playful approach is opportunity to "fall gracefully" into turbulence and to recognize and accept that the sadness of falling is intricately wrapped in the joy of success. We recognize that we are not alone. What has happened to us has happened throughout the whole organization and the entire field. The Whiteheads sense that spiritual vocation is concerned with both positive energy and negativity. Without the possibility of the negative, they suggest we cannot enjoy an all-encompassing, healthy notion of vocation in education, work, and the lives of everyone involved.

## STARTING POINTS FOR FURTHER REFLECTION

1. In his book on vocation, spiritual writer Parker Palmer (2000) comments on the uncertainties of vocation. A wise thinker and a Quaker, Palmer says that "before you tell your life what you intend to do, listen for what it intends to do with you" (p. 3). Did you listen to what your life has told you to do? Do you listen to it now?

2. How do you view your vocation? Is it hard work? Drudgery? A creative event?

3. What challenges you about the notion of vocation as both playful creativity and robust resistance?

## BODY WORK

Accepting the Whiteheads' (1995) view of vocation/creation as creative play challenges those of us who seem driven to think of our vocation as work. It is sometimes difficult to associate vocation with play, frivolity, and fun. The play metaphor suggests the presence of the body itself; and helps us bring to mind connections between one's physical self and one's mind and spirit. Once we accept these connections, we see possibilities for honoring the body in ways that enhance our spiritual lives, to make our lives more whole, and to work towards a more integrated self.

Care of the body is an integral dimension of an adult educator's or trainer's spirituality. This theme is echoed in the writing of such postmodernists as Spretnak (1991) who argue for the full acceptance and integration of the body. To Spretnak, the embodied self that adult educators and trainers bring to life and work is more than text. As we build ourselves mentally, intellectually, and emotionally, we have the potential to build ourselves spiritually. When we are in touch with our bodies' rhythms, seasons, and limits, we come closer to being in touch with our inner spirit. This is our vocation in life.

Being holistic in our practice means being holistic in all of our lives. The congruence among all parts of our being moves us towards a spiritual integration of life, of the unity and purpose in our being, and of the full selves that we bring to work. Our bodies are part of our work, to be cared for as they give and receive. Those who study the body's relationship to the mind and spirit know these parts of our being are intimately linked. Working with, and not against, our bodies is essential for holistic living. Even government and workplace organizations, albeit not for spiritual reasons, promote mind-body wellness and active living. Yet, we want to move beyond health promotion for the sake of physical fitness, reduced absenteeism and illness, decreased stress, and increased productivity. Attending to the body is more than a means to an end; it is a process that makes us fully alive through mind-body connection. Because the spirit is not ethereal, attending to the body attends to the spirit.

In our haste to cultivate our minds we often forget our bodies. But the body, as the ancient Hebrews noted, is a temple —an integral, holistic part of the self. Neglecting the body invites sickness and dysfunction—a broken spirit. The connection of bodywork and movement to the spiritual is not new. Bodywork (see *Journal of Bodywork and Movement Therapies*) refers to a range of physical practices such as fasting, massage, bioenergetics, and therapeutic touch, all of which are ways to physically and mentally revitalize us. Bodywork embraces working, doing a physical ritual, cleansing, celebrating sensuality, and combining meditation and movement. We discuss these below.

> *The monastic Benedictine philosophy Ora et Labora (work and prayer) has long understood that physical work and prayer were one. The Benedictines, and many others, have understood that to fully live the spiritual life, the body*

*and the mind both need to be honored. Consequently, hard physical work plays an important part in Benedictine spiritual practices. In* The Cloister Walk, *writer Kathleen Norris (1996) relates her experiences of living temporarily in a Benedictine monastery. Citing the order's founder, St. Benedict, Norris says that no one shall be excused from kitchen duty. She points out that even the most learned Benedictine scrubs the floors and cleans the tables. No community member is exempt from service, whether that person be the leader of the order or the bell ringer. (p. 7)*

The incorporation of the body into prayer has historical standing in many spiritual traditions. One only has to think how the rituals of genuflecting, kneeling, bowing, and candle lighting are part of Eastern and Western spiritual traditions. Another example is the spiritual practice known as "walking the labyrinth." The labyrinth is a complex pattern, with many pathways. It is engraved in the floor or ground, and one can follow it while contemplating or meditating. One of the oldest known labyrinths is engraved on the stone floor of Chartres Cathedral in France. This labyrinth has been reproduced in places such as Grace Cathedral in San Francisco, and in retreat centers, as a way to encourage seekers to embody their prayer—to bring the body into prayer.

The labyrinth is but one example of how a spiritual tradition has incorporated the body into prayer, and of more fully honoring the body-mind-spirit connections. In walking the labyrinth, the seeker loses a sense of time and lets go of all that holds him or her to earth. The labyrinth is a way to relax the mind and the body, to let go, and to allow the spirit to enter. It is also a reminder that the mind, body, and soul are one.

Fasting to cleanse the body of toxins and heighten one's sensual and spiritual awareness is also not new to spiritual seekers. There are many documented cases of how fasting can contribute to spiritual experiences, although there are also instances of how fasting has been connected with negative body image and eating disorders. Fasting is a way to "break the routine, or better, to heighten one's sensitivity to the routine. It is to dehabituate us to the dailyness" (Smith, 1985, p. 104). Fasting "can also have the effect of providing a space in our life that puts us, for however short a time, into a different rhythm" (p. 104).

Columbia University professor Walker Bynum (1987), in her book *Holy Feast and Holy Fast,* argues that religious women in the Middle Ages used fasting as their only means to gain control in their lives and mastery over their own bodies, in a time when independence for these women was impossible. Their extreme attitude towards their bodies made regular living and eating impossible. Although this instance is extreme, it points to the powerful role our bodies play as sites of learning, spirituality, and politics.

The East has also used many spiritual practices to bring body, mind, and spirit together. One of the better known is tai chi, a pattern of slow controlled movement from one position to the next. Tai chi encourages mindfulness because it pays attention to the moment, in both physical functioning and psychological attitude (Mills, Allen, & Morgan, 2000, p. 39). Tai chi can relieve stress, improve balance, and give a general sense of well-being. Most importantly, it can strengthen the mind and the spirit by bringing those who practice it in touch with their personal body rhythms, range of movement, and breathing patterns. This Eastern attention to the mind, spirit, and body together is somewhat foreign in the West. Western spiritual disciplines often focus only on the mind or spirit—often ignoring the body altogether.

Bodywork can also include reflexology (manipulation of key points in the body) or massage, all which encourage knowing our bodies and listening to the messages they send us. In our age where increasingly virtual participation threatens to undermine our basic sensuality and our physical engagement with our worlds, bodywork such as massage can reawaken and heal the mind, spirit, and body. The popularity of Krieger's (1993) book on therapeutic touch is a prime example of the public's hunger for such healing. Because therapeutic touch is based on a belief that universal energy underlies the world, it involves channeling energy, engaging the spirit, and acknowledging the life forces around us.

The variety of ways the body is incorporated into the practice of spirituality may surprise those just beginning a spiritual journey. However, clearly the body is intricately connected to the spirit. Without attuned appreciation for the body, we deny our full humanity and decrease our potential for a full, rich spiritual life. Deliberate work on the body can be coupled with deliberate imaginative and creative work, recognizing that creativity and spirituality are intricately linked. We come to think of ourselves as a whole, more than either a physical or rational being. Attention to the whole is an aesthetic approach to education.

> *Nancy Roth (2001), an Episcopalian priest, describes her hobby as being "close to God's heart in the garden" (p.33). For Roth, the tending and planting are ways to "discover something about the mind of God" (p. 33). The physical nature of the work is a palpable reminder "that I am created from adamah [earth]. I am not 'apart from' the earth; I am 'a part of' the earth" (p. 34). Yet, even all her own work cannot make the garden or even her own life grow and flourish. For that, Roth says she needs ruach (God's life energy) since she is "not only adamah but also the bearer of God's life-energy." (p. 34)*

## MEDITATION AND CONTEMPLATION

Often people think of meditation and contemplation as "sit still," "be quiet" processes. But, for many, the body is already integrated into the practices of meditation and contemplation that constitute their spiritual disciplines. Meditation is the "spirit's indwelling upon itself" (O'Brien, 1985, p. 182). Without mediation we can never know the "significance of the life-force that throbs within [us]" (p. 182). Meditation enthusiasts claim it to be life-generating, life-renewing, life-focusing, and life-centering. It helps us be more in touch with our own self. Knowing one's self is a precursor for meditation. Mediation may be practiced in solitude or in community, in a serene and peaceful private space such as an office or bathtub, or in a few stolen moments in a busy public area.

Contemplation differs from meditation in that it is "a more passive, receptive process. You don't focus on anything. This increases the chances of moments of contemplation happening (Carrigan, 2000, n. p.). In contemplation you cannot do anything. A unitive moment with a higher power is a gift. Meditation, however, is focusing "on thoughts, on your breath, your posture, a flame, or a mantra" (n. p.). It can lead to contemplation. Contemplation in the form of centering prayer is increasingly common for people trying to develop spiritual disciplines. Contemplative prayer asks those who practice it to be more mindful, to build mind, spirit, and body connections, to increase a sense of sacredness in the body, and to move to a deeper relationship with inner energies. These guidelines for centering prayer are offered by Contemplative Outreach (2000):

1. Choose a sacred word as a symbol of your intent and consent to God's presence and action within you.

2. Sit comfortably and with eyes closed. Settle briefly, then silently introduce the sacred word as your symbol and consent to God's presence and action within.

3. When you become aware of thoughts, return gently to the sacred word.

4. At the end of your prayer period, remain silent with eyes closed for a few minutes.

These guidelines require that you control your breathing, be still, and pay attention to your breath moving in and out. Breathe slowly and deeply. As you breathe in, find a word or phrase you find meaningful (e.g., peace, joy, or happiness) and pray the word or phrase. As you breathe out, imagine the tension and stress leaving your body. Breathe in the love, peace or joy, and exhale your worry.

A form of meditation that has become increasingly popular is guided meditation or visualization. Visualization has its roots in Ignation spirituality and involves beginning with some concrete images and allowing one's imagination to roam freely from these images. Although often used in religious or spiritual settings, educator John Miller (2000) describes how he uses visualization in education classes at the Ontario Institute for Studies in Education/University of Toronto. Miller believes that guided reflection is essential to unleashing creativity and engagement. Both creativity and engagement are important for educational practice, especially for unleashing the imagination. Guided meditation is one way to move beyond the narrow confines of physical reality and to explore your spiritual self, your deepest hopes and dreams, and the essence of your spirituality.

---

## STARTING POINTS FOR FURTHER REFLECTION

Try guided imagery.

Sit or lie down in a comfortable place. Relax your body, starting with your toes and moving to your head. Slow your breathing and be aware that your breath is moving in and out of your body. Imagine yourself in a warm, safe place. Look around. How does it feel to be here? What does it look like? What colors are in the place? Be aware of your emotions. Feel safe, feel warm, and stay there for a while. Try to do this exercise before you begin teaching a class, as a way to open your mind to new ideas, challenges, and possibilities.

OR

Let your body relax. Let your mind wander to a warm and beautiful field. Imagine that your world is pink and green and beautiful and that you are free. Allow your mind to wander. See a wise person coming towards you. Greet and talk to this person. What is being said? How do you respond? As the person moves away, come slowly back into the room. Open your eyes. How do you feel? Could you do this at least once a day to alleviate your stress?

---

# REFLECTIVE READING

Another time-honored way to nurture your spirituality is by reflectively reading "inspirational" texts. Reflective texts give us opportunities to let our imaginations soar and to understand how others have lived a spiritual life and how they have developed their own spiritual disciplines.

The number of such publications is dizzying. However, readers must be careful because some of these so-called inspirational texts are both shallow or self-serving. As well, any person's list of favorites is bound to be idiosyncratic. We offer here some of our own suggestions only as starting points, for those bewildered by the volume of spiritual writing. Writers who have become dear companions on our own spiritual journeys include Madeline L'Engle, Mitch Ablom, Annie Dillard, and Kathleen Norris. As we share these books, we will also classify them by the type of spiritual writing we think they fall into. We have provided a further list in the concluding chapter.

One type of spiritual reading recounts a personal spiritual journey. Among writers in this tradition, Madeline L'Engle interests us. She writes honestly and frankly about her lifetime spiritual journey, with its episodes of joy, fear, relationship challenges, and spiritual ups and downs. *The Rock That Is Higher* (1993) details her painful and spirit-filled recovery from a car accident far from her New York home. Weak and vulnerable in a strange place, she is cared for by friends and yet experiences profound moments of aloneness and fear. Only her deep, abiding relationship with the Divine sustains her. The central motif of L'Engle's book is that many of us do not know where home is, but we continue to search for it. This book is typical of L'Engle's work—rich in feeling and honest in its appraisal of her spiritual journey. It is life-affirming, reflective, and reflexive in style and content. The book challenges the reader's notions of an idyllic, spiritual life full of ecstatic experiences and underscores the embedded spirituality of the everyday world.

The second type of reflective writing is spiritual friendship. Mitch Ablom's (1997) *Tuesdays with Morrie* exemplifies this category. This bestselling, nonfictional account tells how a successful journalist and sports writer becomes reacquainted with his college professor, Morrie Shwartz, who had taught him sociology at Brandeis University in Massachusetts. In his weekly visits with Shwartz, who is dying of Lou Gherig's disease, Ablom hears simple, yet profound views on living and dying. *Tuesdays with Morrie* is about the relationship between an old professor and his middle-aged student, about wisdom in living, and about returning to our roots. In this book a spiritual friendship blooms between two people, which leaves both with a deeper spiritual life. Reading books like this supports the formation of close friendships, and the discussion of significant issues among friends. Ablom's account of his meetings with Morrie affirm that spirituality may become more of an issue later in life than earlier and may become more significant in times of sickness and death.

A third type of spiritual writing is the mystical. Typically nature mysticism, these accounts retell powerful experiences of the Holy. Among these modern-day mystics is Annie Dillard, a writer whose feet are firmly planted on the ground, yet who is able to communicate her Thoreau-like experiences of being at one with the natural world. In *Holy the Firm* (1984) and her previous work *Pilgrim at Tinker Creek* (1974), she writes about her own spiritual life, how she experiences creation, and how she communes with nature. She asks questions about time, reality, life, death, and a higher power. In her *Teaching a Stone to Talk* (1982), Dillard challenges us to discover and pursue our dreams, allowing them to teach us how to live in our own "right" ways, without using these dreams as escape mechanisms.

The fourth type of spiritual writing is centered in monastic, retreat-like experiences. In *The Cloister Walk* (1996), Kathleen Norris, a Protestant laywoman, writes about living for almost two years in a Benedictine monastery. In poetic prose she recounts her deep spiritual awakening in the monastery, which itself embodies spirituality, sacred images, questions, rhythm, and life. *The Cloister Walk* moves beyond rules and rigid religious precepts to depict the depth and beauty of spiritual life nurtured by monastic order and rhythm. Her time spent in the monastery is crucial for her soul, her life, and her spirit. It is time given to her spirit. This book may interest those who retreat to their own quiet places, whether apartments or the country, to practice meditation and solitude.

These four selections represent some of the more authentic and fulfilling spiritual reading currently available. We believe reading about the spiritual lives of others is a prime way to discover we are not alone in our spiritual journeys. This type of reading can stimulate our own spiritual practices and help us see the variety of ways spirituality is lived out.

Because these books have been written in a reflective and thoughtful way, the way we read them ought to honor the way in which they were written. Franciscan Carl Koch (1990) suggests how a reader might do this. Begin by finding a comfortable and sacred space in which to read. You can use candles, music, or meaningful symbols around you to create a warm atmosphere. If this is not a physical space, it might be a quiet mental space on a bus or subway. Then open yourself to pray the reading. Read meditatively, allowing yourself to relish its "feelings, meanings, and concerns" (p. 10). Read one passage at a time, slowly and reflectively, allowing for immersion in a passage and for comprehension. Allow your mind to wander into associations and connections. Do not rush to cover content; instead, allow yourself to be imbued with the writer's intent, rhythm, and meaning and, in so doing, to create your own.

This is a different kind of reading and reflecting than most of us do, so it may be a challenge. We suggest that, if you don't know where to start, you begin with the spiritual reading series *Companions for the Journey* (e.g.,Vinje, 1990). This series provides selections from some spiritual writers such as Julian of Norwich, and then specific reflections, questions, prayers, artistic responses such as painting and drawing, imaging, and journal writing. These guided books are brief and broken down into manageable chapters for busy people who do not have a lot of time but who want intellectual stimulation and reflection.

## JOURNAL WRITING

Along with absorbing the spiritual lives of others through reading, adult educators and trainers can take advantage of journal writing to encourage thinking deeply about their own spiritual journey. Journals help one examine one's spiritual life, and have long been utilized as a spiritual practice (Neal, 2000c; Progoff, 1992). Although writing in a journal is not always easy, it can be incorporated into our everyday lives as a way of processing our emotions, enhancing joy, purging negativity and anger, and understanding our relationships with coworkers, a higher power, friends, family, and the natural world.

Miller (2000) points out that using journals to critically reflect on oneself and one's abilities is crucial for educational practice. Journal writing can open doors of creativity inside each of us and make us aware of feelings we did not know we had. Ultimately, our own journals can help us understand ourselves and our lives—our spirituality. The type of journal we suggest here differs from a professional diary or logbook; the subject is spiritual and is intended to combine the personal and professional.

The journal provides a means for adult educators and trainers to reflect critically on their personal and professional lives (English & Gillen, 2001). Journal writing helps us catch the traces of self, make sense of these traces as they become apparent to us in our everyday activity, and come to know and embrace our many shifting selves and their conflicts of love and hate. Journal writing is one way to understand who we are, why we exist, what energizes or exhausts us, and what we need to feel fulfilled. Journal writing is an engaged process that enables a writer to name, sort, and frame problems. One simple way to begin is to first write about specific problems, dilemmas or places of tension in your day. Follow this by identifying issues or themes in the writing; then try to reframe the problem to get on with your life in a more constructive way.

As part of the process of introducing a journal-writing strategy to our lives, we need to think about whether we have used writing to understand ourselves. And, if we have, was it effective? We may have used journals for experiences as diverse as recording workplace events, taking field notes as part of action research, writing for personal development, and documenting readings for academic purposes (see Boud & Walker, 1998; Wlodkowski, 1999).

Progoff (1992), a Jewish writer, gives us a clear example of how journal writing can aid one's spiritual journey. Progoff developed a journal-writing process for adults that he describes as "an instrument for self-guidance, to crystallize the decisions they need to make, to identify their goals, and to find the meaning of their own unique life" (foreward). Progoff studied under developmental psychologist Carl Jung. As a result, he developed the *intensive journal method,* which encourages writers to explore the deepest parts of themselves. Fundamentally, he says there are many ways to write in a journal. These include imaginary dialogues with other persons, reflections about the body, reconstructions of personal history, dreams, and narrations of recent situations in your life. Each subsection has a different intent and each requires something different of the writer. The goal of the Progoff journal-writing system is to promote inner peace. This method is intensive, yet promising for those interested in examining their own issues.

A second method of journal writing, developed by Cameron (1992), has become immensely popular. It is called the *morning pages.* Simply put, "the morning pages are three pages of longhand writing, strictly stream of consciousness" (pp. 9–10). Cameron calls the morning pages a way of creative recovery. Writing three pages every day is a way to start journal writing because it forces writing, even if the results are not always lucid or meaningful. For Cameron, writing morning pages is a clearing experience. Some may find it a way to move beyond the fear of writing. Although writing three pages of whatever comes sounds simple, the morning pages are an entire process to help the aspiring journal writer begin and continue writing.

A third journal-writing method—created by Berthoff (1987)—is the dialectical notebook, or the use of two pages facing each other. On the left page, you write the "observations, sketches." On the facing page, you write notes on these notes, responses, and comments. This process encourages reflection through journal writing.

Of course, writing about one's self does not come easily, even to many adult educators and trainers who are prolific writers in their occupation. Yet, Berthoff says that "anybody concerned with working out ideas could, should, must be— willy-nilly—a writer, because writing provides the easiest means of carrying out . . . an audit of meaning. Writing as a way of knowing lets us represent ideas so that we can return to them and assess them" (p. 11). An audit of meaning is "a continuing effort to review the meanings we are making in order to see further what they mean" (p. 12). An audit of meaning forces us to consider and explore our deepest feelings and desires, so that we might know what gives our life meaning. Journal writing through the dialectical notebook encourages us to write and analyze what we are writing.

Fear is an integral and expected part of writing a spiritually focused journal. There may be a fear of being soft, silly, or self-indulgent, or of having someone else read your first draft jumblings. For many, the self-consciousness of written spiritual reflection vanishes with practice. Remember, you are in good company. Wise and influential thinkers including Thomas Merton and Henri Nouwen were diligent spiritual journal writers. Another fear is that journal writing can be used unethically to encourage reflection in adult learners and then be read by another. This fear is not unfounded. Given the critiques most of us have endured of our writing, often from past schooling experiences, it may be difficult to write freely especially revealing highly personal reflections. It is critical the educators respect the privacy of learners' journals and remember that whatever pages instructors ask to see will be written with an audience in mind.

*Etty Hillesum (1985), a Jewish woman who died in Auschwitz, recorded all her thoughts, feelings, and ideas in her journal,* An Interrupted Life. *Hillesum documents her transition from an independent and worldly woman into one who is brave and who has incredible spiritual depth. Etty wishes to have the strength to write her story, to record all that has happened to these Jewish people, and to bring not only her intellect to the other prisoners but also her "thinking heart" (p. 236).*

---

## STARTING POINTS FOR FURTHER REFLECTION

Try journal writing.

1. Challenge yourself to write without stopping for three pages (Cameron, 1992). Allow yourself to have a stream of consciousness. Suspend belief and keep writing without thinking too much. Do this every morning for a week. Reread the pages, and think about what you have written. Is this who you are, what you are about? What themes are there in this text? What are the main issues that arise?

2. Take a few minutes before you go to bed to write a gratitude journal (Breathnach, 1995). This journal should contain notations on all that you are grateful for.

---

# RITUALS

Often a helpful part of spiritual development is to ritualize practices such as journal writing early in the morning or contemplation in the evening. Deliberate attention to rituals is an integral and ancient part of spiritual journeying. Creating personal rituals or recognizing rituals one already has help create a rhythm and synergy in one's life. Birthday celebrations, waving goodbye, and regular mealtimes are simple everyday rituals. Work can also be a ritual.

In writing about the Benedictine tradition, Norris (1996)

describes how Benedictines manage to ritualize and make holy even the most mundane tasks. They create ceremonies and rituals that guide eating, sleeping, dressing, and worshipping. They pray at dusk and dawn, sing hymns, read psalms, eat in silence while scripture is read, and have recreation time. She compares this ritual and mindfulness to the artist's life, saying that both the monk and the artist try to "pay close attention to objects, events, and natural phenomena" that are too often overlooked because they are ordinary. The ritual and mindfulness are ways to sanctify the ordinary, to give thanks, and to make holy the small things of life.

As theologian Driver (1991) has pointed out, rituals help make each day holy. They are ways of knowing our own selves and of honoring what we have been doing in our own life. Driver writes that humans have a deep longing for rituals and he notes that without ritual "a society can scarcely exist, let alone be good" (p. 8). Rituals such as family meals, birthday celebrations, and funeral rites shape us, and we are shaped by them. Rituals legitimate changes, mark events, and allow the inexpressible to be conveyed in movement, song, and gesture. But Driver (1991) also points out that ritual can be used against us, such as religious rituals that exclude women or that celebrate violence and promote hatred.

Hughes and Quinn (1993) also explain that "ritual is a powerful medium of expression which publicly marks boundary or threshold moments in people's lives, clarifies and intensifies the experience being named and celebrated, expresses change of status, establishes new relationships, alleviates some of the peril of the unknown, and gives permission for new ways of being and acting as one continues on the journey" (pp. 91–92). Driver (1991) rues the fact that we do not have more rituals. He says our bodies cry out for rituals to soothe our minds, bodies, and souls. For many of us, rituals are part and parcel of our lives. These include eating with family, telling stories to each other, enjoying family vacations, and taking routine trips to pick up the kids. All legitimate parts of our lives can become rituals to be celebrated and attended to in the workplace or at home in ways that honor our moments of success, failure, and happiness.

*A powerful example of food as symbol, ritual, and hospitality is found in the Danish film,* Babette's Feast *(Axel, 1989). Fleeing the French Revolution, Babette finds her way to a village on the coast of Denmark where austerity and an absence of earthly goods prevail. Two dour Christian women and their father take her in. For 14 years, Babette cooks their bad food and honors their simple ways. Her only connection to France is a lottery ticket that a friend purchases for her each year.*

*One day, Babette wins the lottery. Astonishingly, she decides to spend it all on an exotic gourmet feast for the family who gave her asylum and their ascetic community. When the banquet begins, the mood is somber with the silent judgment of diners appalled at the sinful indulgence represented by the feast. But as dish after exquisite dish is brought from the humble kitchen, the ambience begins to change, and joy slowly spreads through the grave gathering. Conversation becomes animated, and old resentments and self-righteousness begin to melt under the power of a delicious shared meal. The film ends with the little community, having talked to dawn, holding hands in the village square before parting. Later it is revealed that Babette was formerly a famous Parisian chef, who has exhausted her personal talents and finances in a loving gift of food as ritual.*

Such stories challenge North American presumptions about isolationism, materialism, and greed. Relationships between food, friendship, giving, and communion seem linked to spiritual purpose and substance. For those connected with a church, synagogue, or some other form of institutionalized religion, food imagery is imbued with religious overtones. For most societies gathering in secular or sacred celebration, feasting is an important marker of connection and communion.

Other possibilities for ritual include responding in affirmative ways to our relationship to the natural world. Just as spirituality must include honor of the body, it must also include honoring the natural world and acknowledging—through ritual

—our own personal relationship with it. For Clover, Follen, and Hall (1998), the recognition of the intimacy of our connection to the environment is important. The modern Western mindset has encouraged the molestation of the land and creation and allowed the destruction of the environment, further isolating us from the earth to which we belong. In part, this isolation has exulted the mind and further bifurcated the mind and body, allowing us to think we can destroy our lives. Yet, the earth is not a dead thing. It is alive; and, by nurturing our connections to it, we can build our own spiritual reserves.

The great traditions have always respected and recognized the environment and its spiritual nature in ritual. Rituals that honor the natural world include being mindful every day that the earth around us is precious, thinking explicitly of the earth as an important piece of our spirituality and of humans not at the center or apex of creation but just one part of it. This may mean "field trips" to green spaces if we do not live near them. It may mean blessing the earth or the water, gardening, hiking, or caring for the environment as a means of touching all of creation. Ultimately, we are working to develop our own spirituality.

A number of activities seem essential for our own spiritual growth and development. These include ritualizing our day, acknowledging the positive and negative aspects of our lives, and bringing special attention to the everyday events of greeting colleagues and learners. Ritual is a simple way to become more in touch with the routines of every day and with our own responses to our every days. Rituals also help us build relationships; they strengthen our sense of self and other. Ritual is a way of incorporating our senses into living.

## CULTIVATING SOUL FRIENDS

One established way of developing our spiritual lives is by fostering a spiritual friendship or finding a kindred spirit to accompany us on our journey. Spiritual friendship is sometimes known as mentoring, or by the Celtic word *anamchara*. This soul friend (see also Leech, 1977) knows you well and wants you to succeed in your spiritual quest. This spiritual friend is there when you fall and is also making a spiritual journey. Making time for a relationship with a person with whom we have an affinity is in and of itself a spiritual connection or discipline. An obvious question arises: Whom do I know who is soulful or spiritual? To answer this question, Edward Sellner (1990) offers a sevenfold description of the characteristics of a soul friend. We adapt them here to the life of an adult educator or trainer.

1. The first characteristic of soul friends is not that they are magical or mystical, but that they are mature. Mature people have faced their own questions, crises, and suffering.

2. Soul friends hear what we are saying, have compassion, and care for us without judgment.

3. Soul friends have genuine respect for others, which develops from their own ability to know and attempt to understand their own stories. This means that soul friends are reflective and self-reflective.

4. Soul friends hold your stories told in confidence; they respect you enough not to tell your story to others.

5. Soul friends self-disclose. Soul friends tell you their own stories of joy and sorrow, of ups and downs. Soul friends are reciprocal friends.

6. Soul friends reflect on their own personal questions and relationships, which can include relationships with a higher power.

7. Soul friends see when things are wrong for you, know when your spirit is disturbed and upset, when you need help, and what type of support you can give and receive.

No one person may have all these characteristics of a soul friend. Nor is there an exact way of being a soul friend. Soul friends guide you on a spiritual journey, supporting you in your struggles and in your search for spiritual disciplines that suit your personality and your life.

*The acknowledgments page of many books provides a fascinating glimpse into the networks and friendships that sustain and nurture a writer. Driver (1991) wrote in his book: "If not to read one's manuscripts and candidly respond, what are old friends for?. . . . These friends are given by heaven to guide me." (p. x)*

## SUMMARY

In summary, we all might attend to matters of the spirit in many ways, difficult as they may seem. The first and most important is examining or embracing a sense of vocation as playing in a creation that is still in process. This sees the world as our oyster, a place where we have purpose and mission, a place where what we say makes a difference. This is our worldview and our purpose. Second, to extend the Whiteheads' play metaphor, we need to write our stories, to bring our bodies to the playground, to develop rituals, to journal, and to nurture our significant friendships so that we do have soul friends and guides with us.

# CHAPTER 4

## Spirituality in the Work of the Educator and Trainer

The Irish poet Seamus Deane (1977) once wished that "the weight of / learning would bring me down / to where things are done" (p. 43). In this chapter we discuss ways that the theory and the conceptual work on spirituality can be brought into the everyday world of practitioners. We explore how spirituality can be interwoven with education and training practice, and we discuss the tensions and dilemmas of promoting spirituality as part of pedagogy.

### LANGUAGE AND PERSPECTIVE

Before we begin, we wish to make a note about language. In this chapter, and indeed throughout the entire book, we use words often reserved for religious spaces. Some of these words include *sacred, reverence, mystical, holy ground, soul, ethical,* and *heart.* This language seems to have been rendered suspicious by the marketplace. One of our goals for this book is to reclaim this language for the everyday practice of adult education or training. We also mean to reclaim these words from the exclusive use of churches, synagogues, and mosques, and to reintegrate them into the vernacular from which they came. One only has to recall that the word *holiday* was derived from the concept of "holy day" to remember that not so long ago these words were commonplace, certainly not in the exclusive domain of religion.

Adult educators and trainers who hope to incorporate

spirituality into their practice face many challenges. One challenge in working with learners is to understand the transitions that must be made when thinking and speaking about spirituality and spiritual topics in adult education and training. We suggest that adult educators and trainers move from a stance of tolerating to a stance of authentically respecting what another person has to say and what that person chooses to do. Similarly, we suggest that courtesy is not sufficient. Rather, adult educators and trainers might think of their practice in terms of hospitality: a spirit of welcoming and inviting others into our spaces. This is a process not removed from the world, but very much in it.

> *Dietrich Bonhoeffer (1962), Lutheran, German pastor, theologian, and patriot, was killed by the Nazis for resisting their regime. The collection of his letters and papers from prison echoes his emphasis on living one's beliefs in the every day. Bonhoeffer stressed that only by living completely in this world can one learn to believe: "Later I discovered and am still discovering up to this very moment that it is only by living completely in this world that one learns to believe . . . taking life in one's stride, with all its duties and problems, its successes and failures." (p. 42)*

## BRINGING SPIRITUALITY TO OUR TEACHING

Adult educators and trainers can go beyond merely acknowledging the other to honoring that other. This means more than knowing others. It means to, in a spirit of active love, "honor the ground they walk on." This includes honoring their space as holy ground that should be treated with care and respect. These movements are not just rhetorical—they signify a change of thinking about how we are present to and interact with others. Specifically, they signify a reclaiming of the spiritual aspects of our being, a naming of the important parts of our lives. Below, we examine and give examples of several ways of bringing spirituality into teaching.

## Holistic Practice

We begin with the need to work from a holistic perspective in our teaching. By holistic, we mean both educators and learners are more than the sum of their physical, emotional, social, or cognitive parts. New Zealand–based educator Heron (1999) explains that holistic education incorporates the spiritual and is an integral part of how we educate. For him, every aspect of life is spiritual, and spirituality is always life.

Holistic learning or, as Heron (1999) calls it, "whole person" learning, engages the person as a "spiritually, energetically and physically endowed being encompassing feeling and emotion, intuition and imaging, reflection and discrimination, intention and action" (p. 1). Whole person learning assumes that adult educators and trainers are also involved in whole person living, or that they cultivate lifestyle practices that support their whole person. One of the often neglected aspects of living holistically is spirituality.

The belief that educators should incorporate a spiritual and holistic perspective into their teaching is not new. Spirituality has been practiced, hand in hand with professional work, for such a long time that we sometimes take it for granted. While the names change, the concepts remain the same. Some other names that describe the link between spirituality and adult education or training include "renewal of personal energy" (Hunt, 1992); "holistic learning" (Boud & Miller, 1996); and "aesthetic education" (Harris, 1987). Even John Dewey used the term *experiential education* in what we believe is a spiritual way (Dewey, 1959). For Dewey, the insights gained from experience itself actually "en-spirited" and guided every aspect of living—making education itself a political act focused on the democracy of humanity. It kept Dewey's eyes focused towards earth and not towards heaven.

Holistic education practices involve learners, teachers, and the learning environment itself. For example, a number of scholars affiliated with the Ontario Institute for Studies in Education (OISE)/ University of Toronto have asked how spirituality can be developed and fostered and how it might include a spiritual dimension. These scholars, such as Hunt (1992), Miller (1993, 2000), Denis and Richter (1987), and Griffin (1997), have written prolifically about the implications of a holistic practice of education for the learner, institution, and the educator.

OISE/University of Toronto graduates, including MacKeracher (1996), have continued the line of research and contributed to a richer insight into holistic teaching and learning processes. MacKeracher's book, *Making Sense of Adult Learning,* turns attention to all the ways that adults need to facilitate learning. She focuses on the emotional, cognitive, social, physical, and spiritual aspects of the learner in her discussion. MacKeracher sees learning as a kaleidoscope where "the characteristic shape and colour of the separate pieces matter much less than the combinations created as colours and shapes mingle" (p. 243). She advocates using metaphors, recording dreams, and writing journal entries as ways to help educators and learners increase their self-understanding and self-knowledge.

A holistic approach sees the spiritual health and well-being of the learner and the educator as important to education. Holistic perspectives embrace multiple views of educational practice and believe that a breadth of educational dimensions is important. They view the practice of personal spiritual exercises as intricately related to the everyday practice of education. From holistic perspectives, the division between personal and professional is artificial (MacKeracher, 1996). In fact, given the multidimensional definitions of spirituality we discussed in Chapter 1, a true spirituality is not only personal but contributes to an outpouring of generosity to others. Below we examine several ways that educators can be more holistic in their teaching.

## Cultivating Learning Environments as Sacred Spaces

As educators and trainers, we have a special role to play in the cultivation of a truly sacred or spiritual learning environment. This process involves many things, but one of the most important is examining what we mean—and what others have meant—by the word *spirit.* As always, one way to understand any word is to examine its etymology. The etymology of the word *spirit* can be traced to the Latin word *spiritus,* which means breath. The word in Greek, *pneuma,* means air or wind. The word in Hebrew is *ruach* or spirit. The word in Chinese is *ch'i* or vitality-spirit. These words obviously sound different, but they have one essential commonality. In every language, the notion of spirit implicitly carries with it the idea that spirit is something we cannot live without. Our spirit fills our being, and is all of us. It is our life, our sustenance.

Our spirit is a place where the sacred part of us may live—in fact, must live. We must create a space for the spiritual. The theme of sacred spaces is hardly new. It has been taken up by a variety of writers, including Heron (1998), who suggests that any understanding of the sacred must promote the connection with a "sacred space."

> *A sacred space is much more than a geographical entity. Sacred space is created not so much with things as with attitudes and dispositions. A space can never be embodied with a sacred nature until it is inhabited with particular thoughts, people, and care. A simple story from Henri Nouwen (1986), a giant of spirituality in the 20th century, illustrates this statement. When Jean Vanier speaks about that intimate place, he often stretches out his arm and cups his hand as if holding a small, wounded bird. He asks: "What will happen if I open my hand fully?" We say: "The bird will try to flutter its wings, and will fall and die." Then he asks again: "But what will happen if I close my hand?" We say: "The bird will be crushed and die." Then he smiles and says: "An intimate place is like my cupped hand, neither totally open nor totally closed. It is the space where growth can take place." (p. 34)*

A sacred space is an area conceptually sanctified or separated from the everyday world, often for the purpose of worship. Obviously, as Davidson (1988) says, all religions have sacred spaces—holy places of communication between humans, gods, spirits, and the forces of nature. The importance of the place as sacred is also underscored in writing on spirituality and adult education or training. For instance, Vogel (2000) refers to the importance of place in Norris's work on sacred places (see Chapter 3 of this book). For Vogel and Norris, there is a holy ground on which any educator walks in the presence of others, that respects those others. Being mindful of one's power as a teacher or a leader is especially important. This is best illustrated with the words of a 13th-century German mystic Mechthild of Magdeburg,

> Mechthild of Magdeburg came to live at the great convent at Helfta in her old age. Prior to that she had been a Beguine, one of a group of laywomen living in a community and working with the poor. Her collection of sayings and thoughts were compiled in a book called Flowing Light of the Divinity (1991). Mechthild's run-ins with those who did not respect her, and who misused their power, are discussed in her book. She offers these words of advice to the other women at Helfta, especially to the leaders: "There lies great terror in power. When someone says: 'You are our prelate or our prior', God knows, dear, you will be tempted to the fullest extent, so you should prostrate yourself with great humility . . . so that you may help . . . all your brothers and sisters who have been entrusted to your care" (p. 167). She goes further to tell her readers about how they should act to subordinates: "You should receive all complaints compassionately and give all counsel faithfully" (p. 169). Hers is a servant leadership that encompasses the command to wash the disciples' feet. "You should visit the infirmary . . . You should clean the sickrooms . . . You must stand by them" (p. 168). Finally she advises, "You should have the eyes of an eagle to see and watch your subordinates in God, lovingly, not angrily." (p. 169)

This holy ground and the holiness of all of life are also underscored in the popular resurgence of Celtic spirituality (Mitton, 1996). At least part of this resurgence is because Celtic spirituality connects spirituality to everyday life in a way modern humans long to emulate. The Celtic church reclaims earthy images as both spiritual and as part of everyday messiness.

Rather than isolate spirituality from life, spirituality is fully embraced as part of life, earth, and relationship. The Celts also celebrate women, such as St. Brigid of Kildare, as bishops. Because the Celtic church honored the earth, people, and relationships, it did not create walls of tension between the sacred and the secular. Columba, an Irish monk, was known to have prayed "Let me do my daily work, gathering seaweed, catching fish, giving to the poor./ Let me say my daily prayers, sometimes chanting, sometimes quiet, always thanking God" (cited in Mitton, p. 45). This is a place modern humans can live quite comfortably.

Eastern spiritual traditions also have worked to break down the wall between the secular and the sacred. This is even true in music. As the Ravi Shankar Foundation Website (Shankar, 2000) suggests, *"Nada Brahma—Sound is God."* The core of Ravi Shankar's music has been a spirituality which instantly touches the listener. Shankar talks about how everything on earth is recycled. The earth is 200 million years old—the Alps, the water, the air. Billions of people have breathed the same air. Knowledge keeps everything fresh. That is why you can keep recycling the same creation. The earth is a sacred space.

Sacred space, according to Vella (2000), consists of several elements, the first of which is *dialogue*. Vella says that "the heart of a spirited epistemology is respect for dialogue" (p. 11). She holds that sincerity about engaging in dialogue means that the teacher is not an expert on everything. However, Vella does not mean the teacher is vacuous, rather that educational experiences are designed in ways that listen to adult learners' experience and knowledge base and build on what is known to help understand what is new.

Such dialogue first means a considerable amount of planning. Second, it means that the educator or trainer is intricately involved in the planning, facilitating, and evaluating of the educational experience. This approach is distinctive because its starting place is reverence, not just tolerance, of the other person. It is grounded on a profound understanding that the other person is to be honored and respected—that he or she is on holy ground. It is about "rooting education in the practices of openness, attentiveness to experience, and sensitivity to the world" (Glazer, 1999, pp. 11–12).

Second, Vella (2000) suggests that a strong sense of *respect* for learners is important when creating sacred space. Respect needs to be both part of the design phase of adult education and training, and part of the interactions between teacher and student. Respect means, first and foremost, asking about learners' needs and really listening to the answers.

> *Gabriel Marcel (1949), 20th-century French philosopher, wrote extensively on the notion of presence: "Though it is hard to describe in intelligible terms, there are some people who reveal themselves as 'present'—that is to say, at our disposal . . . presence is something which reveals itself in a look, a smile, an intonation or a handshake." (pp. 25–26)*

Our respect for our learners is conveyed in our tone and the ways we speak to them. Respect is also embodied in how we handle conflict. As in any human-to-human contact, negotiating differences respectfully is one of the greatest challenges of being an educator or trainer.

In a postmodern context, respect is carried to a new level. An appreciation for difference is called for. In this context, inclusion, interrelationships, and nexus are valorized as key parts of being in the world. Difference is a challenging concept when one considers how many spiritualities are vying for recognition and acceptance, in some cases challenging long-held beliefs in authority and institutions. The issue of difference cannot be overlooked in a discussion of spirituality. Postmodernism calls us to move beyond the dualisms of good and bad, spirituality versus religion, and to recognize the many ways of fostering our search for meaning or spirituality. We have to "cultivate a high tolerance for difficulty, uncertainty and error" (Usher , Bryant, & Johnson, 1997, p. 25), which may mean a radical repositioning of our worldview.

We may never understand the profound impact a simple choice we make will have on others. Translated into educational practice, adult educators and trainers must consider their spiritual path as they conduct their teaching and living, no matter how small choices may seem. We may never know how our smallest decision may be connected to a larger plan. Sometimes our small parts of the plan add up. Perhaps, our lives and our actions are not so unimportant. We must be diligent to act well, even if we cannot see or understand the fruit of our actions.

When the events of the everyday happen, seemingly here and there, it is impossible to be certain if they are part of some larger plan. Neither can we be certain when "spiritual prompts" lead us towards certain actions and away from others. Perhaps, as good teachers, we should consider that these actions might be arranged into an unknown plan. None of us, obviously, is always capable of seeing the big picture. Our proper response may simply be diligence as we carry out our responsibilities in the little bit of picture we see, especially since we may never know how important each of our decisions may be. In fact, as adult educators or trainers we might even work better if we avoid making any judgments about the relative value of the decisions we make—one may seem huge, but be small; one may seem small, but turn out large. Instead, we must consider each decision and each action of our lives to be of utmost importance.

Vella (2000) suggests that *accountability* is a third way to convey respect. The teacher is accountable to the learner for the "design" of the educational experience. Therefore, designing education experiences is an act of reverence with the learner foremost in the educator's mind. The educator and the learner are in "a dynamic reciprocal unity" (p. 14). This accountability precludes sloppiness, inadequate planning, and ensures that all do their best work. Vella's wisdom is obvious. It simply makes sense to us as adult educators and trainers that the triumvirate of respect, dialogue, and accountability will effectively help adult educators and trainers create sacred spaces in the learning environment.

Expressions of fear, anxiety, depression, and guilt are integral parts of the human condition. Because this is true, they are also parts of any learning space. Consequently, the educator or trainer's ability to embrace what some may call "negative" emotions becomes an important role modeling for learners.

*Palmer (2000), leading spiritual writer, tells poignant tales of his own deep despair, when he suffered a dark, clinical depression, and of the friends who loved him back to health. He says, "Twice in my forties, I spent endless months in the snake pit of the soul. Hour by hour, day by day, I wrested with the desire to die, sometimes so feeble in my resistance, that I practiced ways of doing myself in" (p. 58). His engagement with his dark hours is insightful since he is so well published and respected, and since he has been able to write about this depression as well as his attempts to integrate (not separate) this experience into his teaching and writing.*

Whitehead and Whitehead (1994) point out that negative emotions help us understand that life is complex and challenging. In the words of the Whiteheads, we need to know that "to be human is to be aroused" (p. 3). Anger challenges us to right a wrong; it calls us to decisive action to protect those we judge to be in genuine harm; and it leads us to pursue justice. Anger also alerts us to those issues for which we have most passion. If we see ourselves as people of personal dignity, guilt and shame may actually remind us of the shape of our best self. They support our sense of integrity, while depression can ready us for mature grieving and change. The ability to honor these emotions in our training and educating is very important.

---

## STARTING POINTS FOR FURTHER REFLECTION

Think about your own life journey. Consider an emotion that is sometimes a problem for you (e.g., anger, shame, guilt, or depression). Trace that emotion through your life. Have you improved your ability to deal with it? Do you have hopes for how you could deal with it better? (Whitehead & Whitehead, 1994, pp. 186–187)

---

A further discussion of how spaces of learning might be constructed is given in Palmer's (1998) *The Courage to Teach*.

Palmer describes the type of educational space best described in terms of paradoxes. These paradoxes or tensions help us describe the negotiation that occurs while grounding one's teaching in a spirituality of everyday life. These paradoxes have a great impact upon the teaching and learning space and, obviously, care must be taken to create them:

- The space must be both open and structured. By this, Palmer means that a space should be free enough to encourage diversity and complex thinking. Yet, it must be directed enough to avoid chaos and to encourage coherent dialogue. This suggests that the lack of specific direction that sometimes seems to accompany what some adult educators and trainers define as *facilitation* may be a mistake. A good learning experience should have boundaries and direction. Palmer recommends that these boundaries include a need for clear educational materials and the guidance of a clear plan, question, or direction for the class.
- The space should be both welcoming and challenging. By this, Palmer means that a good learning space should balance comfort and risk taking. The learner and educator must feel comfortable enough to want to explore deeper questions and enough risk to be motivated or, as he suggests, "on the edge."
- The space should be inviting for both individuals and the group. By inviting, Palmer means that the group should honor and welcome not only individuals but also the whole group. Palmer recommends a balance between individual expression and group thinking, suggesting that both individuals and group should have space.
- The space should honor both individual stories and stories from the discipline. Palmer believes this caveat is an important consideration for adult educators or trainers who often work from a humanistic framework that seems to focus honor upon the learner. Educators and trainers also need to honor the stories, theories, and ideas of the discipline. Without a "disciplined" content, adult educators and trainers may become therapists instead of teachers.
- The space should support solitude and community building. The learning community needs to provide space for people to

participate as they can and will, not as they must. In all this, the learning community must be respectful.

- The space should welcome both quiet and speech. Palmer supports the need for space and for respect for every learner in the community. Palmer also identifies the need for group quiet so that silence can speak and everyone can hear the other. (pp. 74–77)

Palmer's paradoxes are consistent with a pedagogy that respects the spirit working the space. He identifies and tries to establish four key aspects of space: the physical environment, the conceptual framework, the ground rules, and the emotional climate (p. 73). For those interested, Palmer has written a number of other books that might help people attempting to integrate spirituality into their own work.

Palmer's (1983) *To Know As We Are Known: A Spirituality of Education* is a primer on authentic education that explores how mind and heart can work together in the learning process. The book was an early attempt to move beyond the "bankruptcy" of our current educational models. Palmer writes about "the soul of education" as he explores a lifelong cultivation of the wisdom each of us possesses and can share. As always, to us Palmer's goal is consistent—to benefit others.


## Ethical Beginnings and Ethical Endings

Part of any creation of a sacred learning space is the design of specific learning activities. An inviting ethical beginning sets the stage for the learning experience. Many educators have participants introduce themselves as part of their opening activities. Some go beyond this to include the following invitational openings:

- Open with a "check-in," during which participants one at a time share how they are feeling and what's on their mind as they approach the learning process.
- Open with a sharing of "gifts and needs." Participants take

turns stating what they believe to be the gifts they bring the group, and their needs from the group.

- Open with a few minutes of "centering." Invite each participant to take some moments, after the busy rush to get to the group on time, to breathe, become calm, and focus on the learning to come. Educators might provide a short inspirational or focusing text for participants to reflect on.
- Pass around an object, and ask participants each to share something about themselves that they can connect to the object. One educator brought to the group a small leafy branch in an old wine bottle filled with water. After he spoke of its significance to him, each participant in turn brought forth rich images and stories.

Hogan (1994) holds that educators and trainers spend far too little time on how they end their educational sessions and too much time on beginnings and the middle. Most of us who have been part of planning know that our focus often is centered on invitation into a group rather than on transition out of the group. To Hogan the phrase "ethical ending" means the "planned dissolution of a group" (p. 32), an important way to honor the learner, the educator, and the learning experience. She examines further reasons why ethical endings are important:

- The ethical ending is a way for learners to make a smooth transition out of an educational activity and space devoted to intentional learning, back into their communities of everyday activity. Ethical endings help increase the chance that an ending is not traumatic or upsetting for participants who may have become very attached to each other. This transitional purpose helps the group come to closure and start thinking ahead to the ending of the group.
- The ethical ending honors the fact that humans remember beginnings and endings best. This suggests that adult educators and trainers should pay attention to how learners move in and out of a group and to the rituals that mark this transition. If we are really concerned with the quality of learning, we will be concerned with what learners take away from the group.
- Ethical endings celebrate the affective domain. Because an

ethical ending involves more than left brain activity, it integrates the whole person. An ethical ending involves ritual, imagery and symbolism, emotion, creativity, and imagination.

- The ethical ending celebrates group achievement. When celebration becomes a focus, we are allowed to consider what has genuinely been achieved. This is more than a false celebration of achievement designed to encourage students to give the educator a good rating on a student evaluation form. Instead, it is a genuine attempt to bring together and truly celebrate the group's positive accomplishments.
- The ethical ending links course elements. An ethical ending provides the opportunity to bring together the parts of an educational experience.
- An ethical ending helps translate ideas into action. The ending can be used to name and identify how to actually use what has been learned. In fact, it brings learning full circle and actualizes learning's holistic nature. The ethical ending is an opportunity to help learners plan how to live after they return to their place of practice.

By creating an ethical ending, adult educators and trainers can utilize the rituals discussed in Chapter 3. But ethical endings need to be attended to like any good learning experience. They must be prepared and planned so participants are a full and integral part of the process. Without full participation, an ethical ending lacks integrity. Hokey beginnings and endings encourage participants to distrust the process. Hogan suggests some ways of creating ethical endings:

- Try a photo ritual where each learner brings a photograph or a print into the circle and talks about how this photo relates to the end of the group. Hogan suggests using the Millet painting "The Gleaners" which highlights the motifs of harvesting and completing. This painting effectively suggests both positive and negative emotion and can invite a variety of responses. Participants can easily identify meaningful themes.
- Try a writing ritual. Learners can draw or write a statement capturing something important they have learned, or a mes-

sage to each participant in the learning community. They might share this orally or electronically, on individual personal notes or as contributions to a collective scrapbook. Hogan suggests writing on balloons and then releasing them outdoors (although there are environmental considerations here).

- Try a circle ritual. Participants sit in a circle facing each other. They might pass a special stick or object. One at a time, each person holds the object and shares a few words of reflection or feelings about the learning experience and community. Some educators use a "check-out" process, where participants in small groups or plenary one at a time share some of their feelings, thoughts, and closing learnings. Or, Hogan asks participants to make individual and slow eye contact with everyone else in the group. Each person looks silently at others and says a silent goodbye to them.

Hogan's point is that the ending is an integral part of the learning experience. Indeed, if we take holistic learning seriously and are truly respectful of learners, then we will employ ethical endings.

These ethical beginnings and endings are intended to bring an intentional focus on the importance of the process. They help to honor the learning experience of the participants and enable them to enter and exit smoothly.

## Cultivating Spiritual Intelligence

In the 1980s, Harvard education professor Howard Gardner (1983) popularized his theory of multiple intelligences (MI). Basically, Gardner proposed that there are many more kinds of intelligence than are regularly being tested in our culture, especially our schools. Schools, he suggests, are primarily interested in verbal/linguistic and logical/mathematical intelligences. He sees this as a narrow perspective and suggests that there are at least seven intelligences, a theory that has gained much momen-

tum in the K-12 literature. These include visual/spatial, bodily/
kinesthetic, musical, interpersonal, and intrapersonal intelligence (self-awareness). More recently, Gardner (1999) has added
a new category, that of naturalist intelligence, or a way of com-
muning with nature.

This MI theory, while exciting and novel, may have over-
emphasized and trivialized the whole notion of intelligence. Using their knowledge of quantum physics and physiology, Danah
Zohar and Ian Marshall (2000), for instance, offer a subtle critique of Gardner when they argue that there are basically three
intelligences: spiritual intelligence (SQ, which is our meaning-
making capacity), emotional intelligence (EQ, which is an awareness of our own and other's feelings and is necessary for effective use of IQ), and intellectual intelligence (IQ, which is our
knowledge of factual information, such as quantum physics and
physiology). Zohar and Marshall argue that SQ is necessary to
"address and solve problems of meaning and value. [It is] the
intelligence with which we can place our actions and our lives
in a wider, richer, meaning-giving context, the intelligence with
which we can assess that one course of action of one life-path
is more meaningful than another" (pp. 4–5). Zohar and Marshall say that SQ helps us deal with existential problems, since
it is "our deep, intuitive, sense of meaning and value" (p. 13).

This spiritual intelligence can be incorporated into everyday living as a way to bring our "spiritual issues [into] the . . .
world of active human existence" (Berry, 1988, p. 111), or
exercising a "public spirituality" (p. 110). Berry's public spirituality concurs with descriptions of spirituality presented by
Daloz, Keen, Keen, and Parks (1996) in their book *Common
Fire*. Based on 120 intensive interviews with Americans identified as supporting the common good or practicing "values based
politics in the public sphere" (p. xi), these researchers identified
similar concerns, values, commitments, and backgrounds in
those identified as showing moral and ethical courage in the
course of their everyday life and work. Of those interviewed,
82% indicated that their spiritual influences had significantly
influenced their lifelong commitment to the common good and
a quest for meaning.

The cultivation of a spiritual intelligence for women may be especially important, according to some adult educators and trainers. For instance, in *Gender in Popular Education,* Walters and Manicom (1996) draw attention to the importance of links between spirituality and women's development. They note that spirituality is growing in importance to women "as culturally distinct groups. . . . Women recovering womanist traditions and ethnic collectives, draw on cultural and spiritual symbols in healing and transformative education" (pp. 12–13). It is not clear whether this statement is based on empirical data or personally held knowledge. However, incorporating spirituality into learning is helpful for both men and women.

> Orr (2000) has written about the integration of native traditions into adult education through the recovery of a native symbol, the talking circle. "As Mary Jane, a Cree elder, passed the eagle feather around the circle, an amazing calm came over my students. For weeks they had been wired increasingly tighter by the institutional pressures of assignment deadlines plus family and work responsibilities, but in the context of the talking circle their tensions and anxieties dissipated" (p. 59). The exclusive right of the feather holder to speak in the talking circle is a way of honoring and integrating native ways of knowing.

## Mentoring and Coaching as Spiritual Learning Activity

Promoting mentoring and coaching is a specific way to improve the spiritual dimension of adult education and training. Most recently, Darwin (2000) has argued that mentoring is a mixed blessing in the workplace. She also suggests that using mentoring as a strategy needs further critique and careful consideration. Similarly, our stress in this book on mentoring is not about increasing the bottom line. It is about relationship, support, and increasing the human spirit. We take seriously Fenwick and Lange's (1998) critique that spirituality cannot be marketed; it is not about the bottom line.

Mentoring and coaching, Zachary (2000) says, are highly developed concepts and practices. Daloz's (1999) work on mentoring as an approach to teaching and learning has helped bring a fresh perspective to mentoring. He sees mentoring as reciprocal, with the potential to nurture self, others, and the work world. Sellner (1990) talks of mentoring as a form of soul friending that can weave intricate lives together and help them make sense. Mentoring is neither coaching nor a hierarchical supervisory relationship. It is a reciprocal and dialogical approach to working and learning. Nancy Gehrke (1988) also describes the strong, relational component of mentoring. She uses the metaphor of gift exchange to describe mentorship, capturing the notion that mentorship is a mutual self-giving. Elsewhere, English (2000b) discusses mentoring as a way to promote spirituality. She cites the Antigonish Movement as a prime example, where leaders nurtured a strong sense of power and interdependence among people in the community. They offered care, concern, resources, faith and outreach—helping people reach out to others.

> *The desert monastics of Eastern Christianity were required to have mentors or spiritual guides as part of their faith development. The guide was to impart a word of wisdom to the disciple, who in turn was encouraged to value the word and contemplate how it might be applied to daily life. A story is told of Abba Ammoe, who refused permission for his disciples to walk with him for "fear that, after [hearing] edifying words, irrelevant conversation should slip in." (Ward, 1975, p. 26)*

The reciprocal relationship of mentorship echoes Buber's (1958) classical I-Thou/ I-It distinction. Buber constantly insisted that "All real living is meeting." His work showed that when the other is regarded as It in a functional sense the relationship is defined as a helping relationship, not a mentoring one. An I-Thou relationship facilitates both the personal and professional development of mentor and mentee. This relationship allows the moving upward and onward, simply because someone believes in you.

As Buber says, "The primary word *I Thou* can be spoken only with the whole being. Concentration and fusion into the whole being can never take place through my agency, nor can it ever take place without me. I become through my relation to the *Thou;* as I become I, I say *Thou"* (p. 11). In acknowledging this relationship, Buber also says that the "spirit is not in the I, but between I and Thou" (p. 39). The spirituality of the relationship is the reciprocity that constitutes the relationship. This does not ignore the fact that the teacher is a teacher, nor does it ignore the power dynamics that are part and parcel of any human relationship. It means that adult educators and trainers bring this reverence to all their relationships with learners, since every act of teaching is an act of mentoring.

Adult educators need to practice honoring and respecting learners by using gentle speech, giving helpful and honest critique of the learner's work, being present and available to learners, and preparing carefully and thoroughly for class. These actions convey respect and honor for the relationship. Mentoring can be a means of revitalizing teaching and of promoting a continuous learning culture (Cohen & Galbraith, 1995; Schulz 1995). Mentorship can foster more collaborative communities in education and the workplace that respect new people, new ideas, and new skills while honoring traditions and collective knowledge. However, it is also true that mentoring is fraught with the possibility for abuse of power, and for the control of mentors (Darwin, 2000). These possibilities undergird the need for a more spiritual approach to mentoring, one the embodies the I-Thou relationship, discussed above, one that allows for difference in work styles, values and communication styles, and needs and wants.

## Intuitive Learning

Honoring the intuitive parts of learning is an integral part of honoring the spirituality of learning, since the intuition speaks to the deepest, truest part of ourselves. We follow Marge Denis's (Denis & Richter, 1987) distinction that intuition refers to sudden insights, whereas intuitive learning is "a process extending more or less over time" (p. 25). Intuition is not one type of learning but part of all forms of learning. Although intuition is much overlooked, it is an integral part of any discipline. Not surprisingly, intuition is discussed by V. Griffin, D. Hunt, and John Miller, as well as by Heron and MacKeracher (1996). Intuition is a part of the spiritual in that it is about utilizing all our senses. It is about honoring ways of being, beyond physical and cognitive. The intuitive is an aspect of our selves, but it is difficult to measure or to describe. According to V. Griffin (1987), for intuition to occur, it must be nurtured and supported. The old adage that inspiration only comes to a prepared mind applies here; insights come more clearly to those predisposed to them. As V. Griffin says, "Intuitive learners, like any learners, still must develop a place for the insight or discovery to rest in" (p. 31).

One seminal educational thinker who drew considerable attention to intuition is Alfred North Whitehead (1929; see English & Gillen, 2000b), Cambridge and Harvard mathematician and philosopher. Whitehead's educational theory fostered the dissolution of the division between head and heart. In terms of intuition, Whitehead gave "priority to ways of knowing that move beyond the purely intellectual (knowing about and assessing objectively). . . . Rather than a stress on knowing *about,* Whitehead's thought places primacy on living into the experience through one's intuition. This intuitive knowing values feelings, thoughts, experiences, and invites the knower to fully engage that which is to be known" (English, 2000a, pp. 79–80). The knower is called to stay with an experience, "soaking it up until one becomes saturated with it" (Chia, 1997, p. 87).

In *Women as Learners* Flannery (2000) discusses ways women can improve or practice their intuition. She describes her interviews with participants who practice intuitive skills, through a meditative practice. One participant uses singing as a way to foster her intuitive capacity. Flannery's point seems to be that intuition is about being connected to your body, honoring your subjective experiences, and acknowledging knowing that transcends rational, logical thought.

Denis and Richter (1987) recommend that intuition be interwoven into a whole educational program, not held as a separate strand. This intuitive learning does not exist separately from linearity or rationality; it works in conjunction with them. Intuitive learning honors the senses, the experience and feelings of the learner. Intuition is less a skill that one teaches and more a way of honoring what already exists.

In an adult education or training context, the practitioner can accept as valuable the learning that comes in new ways, apart from rational processes. The educator can recognize and allow learners to name this as how they learn; the educator can foster intuitive learning by integrating centering, visualization, guided imagery, meditation, dream analysis, or synectics into an educational process (V. Griffin, 1997). Intuitive learning is nurtured when time is allocated, as MacKeracher (1996) says, for learners and educators to look for "connections in unlikely places . . . [even though] learners insist that what happens in one place does not relate to another" (p. 197). Denis (Denis & Richter, 1987) describes how she used intuitive learning to weave a tapestry—"dialoguing with what was there: getting in touch with the colors, the texture of the wool and so on, letting what was there reach out to me, giving me direction about how to go on with the design, what colors to use next and so on. I was letting it tell me what it wanted it to become" (p. 27).

It is also possible to cultivate intuitive learning by helping learners look for the big picture, to see patterns that might emerge, and by valuing associations, gut feelings, and knowledge that "just happens." It is also possible to help learners connect with their intuitive capacity by having them call to mind past experiences of when their intuition guided their action. Ask the learners to think about the circumstances that were present, the level of alertness involved, and the learning that occurred.

*Hildegard of Bingen (1985), 13th century Rhineland mystic, was known for a variety of gifts, not the least of which were her poems and her music in which she professed her innermost thoughts. She also had a keen intuitive sense that all of life was a circle and a whole. She spoke to the value of intuition in her learning: "What I do not see I do not know. I see, hear and know simultaneously and learn what I know as if in a moment."*

Part of intuition is acknowledging that insight comes in different shapes and sizes. Hildegard (1987) used metaphor and symbol to understand her world. Here she describes how she understands Divinity: "The Godhead is like a wheel, a whole. In no way is it to be divided because the Godhead has neither beginning nor end. No one can grasp it, for it is timeless" (p. 26).

---

## STARTING POINTS FOR FURTHER REFLECTION

One way to cultivate intuition is to allow for free association. The next time you are with a group of learners and you are dealing with a problem, take 5–10 minutes to try this exercise.

Think about what you are learning and what the problem is. Let your mind wander. What images come to mind? What thoughts arise? What colors are suggested? Where does this lead you? Write your thoughts on paper. Explore what you have written. Is there anything here that you have not seen before? What do you learn from this exercise? (Firestone, 1997, p. 221)

---

## Questioning Purpose, Values, and Congruence

Asking or raising questions is one of the simplest yet most effective teaching strategies, used since the creation of teaching. To a considerable extent, these questions have become their own personal art form of teaching and learning. The point of raising powerful questions is not necessarily to find a specific answer, but to learn to dwell in the questions until, as Rilke (1984) suggests, you live yourself into the answers.

## STARTING POINTS FOR FURTHER REFLECTION

Questioning is often a way of challenging ourselves. "Spirit-works" writer J. A. Neal (2000b) has suggested some questions that she uses to uncover the spiritual in work, especially in her online conversations: What role, if any, has spirituality played in the career choices you have made? How did you come to be interested in integrating spirituality and work? Tell me about a particularly satisfying or meaningful time when you were able to practice one or more of your principles, values, or beliefs at work. Tell me about a time when you had difficulty integrating your spirituality and your work. What are the costs and benefits to you of focusing more on spirituality in your workplace?

---

If raising specific questions seems too direct, teachers might choose a variety of other ways to raise questions. For example, learners might be asked to develop a mission statement and challenged to think about how they find their mission in life.

L. B. Jones (1996) suggests that verbs help us think about what excites us. "The verbs we choose to act on that shed light on who we are" (p. 50). Jones notes the power of verbs to help us think about what we value, what we are really interested in, and find out what we are about. Choose three of these verbs: accomplish, acquire, appreciate, communicate, complete, defend, deliver, educate, express, forgive, give, light, live, love, model, prepare, receive, sacrifice, validate, worship, yield. What verbs would you add to this brief list? Think about what they mean to you in the context of what you value in your life.

## Spirituality of Action

Although it is possible to teach and to promote private spirituality and personal development, that is not the spirituality we described in Chapter 1. We believe that just as the learning cycle and experiential learning theory leads to action, so does spirituality. We support the kind of spirituality that encourages learners to decide what their values are and how these values impact both their dreams and the actions of their everyday lives.

Early 20th-century Nova Scotia labor leader, J. B. McLachlan (Frank, 1999), said he believed "in education for action. I believe in telling . . . the truth about the history of the world, that it does not consist of the history of kings, or lords or cabinets. It consists of the history of the mass of the workers, a thing that is not taught in the schools. I believe in telling . . . how to measure value, a thing that is not taught in any school" (p. 416). McLachlan's ideas capture the spirituality we are thinking of. This spirituality moves individuals to action beyond the learning setting. Though we are not suggesting specific activity, we do believe that effective spiritual education is concerned with more than "printed liberty" (Deane, 1977, p. 43), defined as words about freedom that never are translated into action. It ought to stir individuals to think about what they are doing and how they are doing it, and to look for opportunities in their lives for authentic reaching out to others in care and concern—be it through volunteerism, environmental activism, or tutoring.

In *Maelar's Regard* (1999) Newman focuses directly on education for social action, noting that learning is a way of making meaning and making choices, not just for ourselves but rather for the communal good. The active engagement of adult educators and trainers in social action, which Newman describes, is very close to the spirituality for action that we are talking about in this book. We do not see education as divorced from spirituality nor from action.

Newman's book contains many stories illustrating the deep personal relationships and significant events that influenced his social action work in education, many of which we would call spiritual. The title of Newman's book, for instance, refers to an experience that he had in London in the 1970s. While doing educational outreach work he went to a house for the visually impaired in a disadvantaged neighborhood, to see a Braille class in process. On a wall in the basement of this cramped house, a man named Maeler was energetically painting a multicoloured and multitextured mural. When Newman queried the rapidity with which Maelar was working, he was told the artist was losing his sight and was in a rush to complete the work. The regard, or the look that Maelar gave him, stayed with Newman for life and influenced his belief that we cannot have control over much that happens to us or to our learners—we have only the present. Newman places practice and stories such as these at the center of the book, highlighting the primacy of social action, interrelationship, and class analysis.

Similarly, Foley (1999b), a colleague of Newman's, provides ample cases and examples of adult education and social action. Foley is interested in learning that takes place when adults are involved in voluntary work, social action, and political activity. His work is also rich in case studies. Foley's basic question is how adults can learn liberation stories and not oppression. Foley searches for the connections between learning and struggle. This connection is also the one that we see as important for spirituality, which must have an outward, liberating focus.

## Assessing the Spiritual Dimensions of Your Teaching

Adult educators and trainers who really care will likely evaluate their practice rigorously, especially those who take seriously the ethical mandate of incorporating spirituality into their work. We offer a list of questions that an adult educator or trainer might ask in evaluating personal effectiveness. Our list is adapted from a list compiled in 1991 by Rolph:

• Do I encourage a questioning attitude towards the self? Does my teaching challenge the learners to ask questions of ultimate meaning, such as: Who am I? and How do I relate to others? Does my practice help learners interpret purpose and meaning for their lives?

- Does my teaching encourage the development of a sense of worth and a respect for the human dignity of others?
- In my teaching, do I encourage the use of the imagination? Do I provide periods for reflection and inner exploration?
- Does my teaching encourage learners to look beyond the ordinary to the transcendent?
- In my courses, do I integrate religion, literature, poetry, art, and music, and help students search for the meaning and value that they contain?
- Do I encourage students to identify and own their particular faith stance?
- Do I give students breathing room and space to create their own meanings from the learning experience?
- Do I provide opportunities for learners to share what they are thinking and feeling, including their negative thoughts?
- Do I practice being caring and concerned for students?

The difficulties in incorporating spirituality into education become clear when one reads Professor Van den Blink's (1999) account of the death of spirituality in a Protestant theological seminary, where it would seem reasonable to assume that there would be an emphasis on spirituality. Furthermore, Van den Blink observes that students in practical theology (religious education, pastoral work, homiletics, chaplaincy, youth work) know they are treated with disdain by those who have intellectual pursuits such as scripture study. "Ministry was for those who did not have the intellectual gifts for doctoral study" (p. 2). So, if spirituality is not a given in theological education settings, it is certainly not a given in all educational institutions.


# SUMMARY

In this chapter, we have examined some ways adult educators and trainers can bring spirituality to bear on their teaching and learning. Ultimately, we want to promote the creation of holistic learning in our educational work, learning that incorporates the thinking, willing, and feeling capacities in all of us.

## STARTING POINTS FOR FURTHER REFLECTION

Ex-Jesuit John J. McNeill (2000) describes his own spiritual journey as one where "as my body grows older, my spirit becomes younger" (p. 1). He talks of the spirit God has given him and the grace to be continuously aware of a longing in his heart for a greater intimacy with God. McNeil's awareness of God is based on what he is deprived of, what he needs and doesn't have, what he is yearning for, what he has a hunger and thirst for and has not achieved. He prays the *New York Times* daily, formulating a prayer appropriate to every headline and article. In this way, he strives to let his prayer reach into the whole world. Have learners model his example.

Suggest to learners that they spend some time thinking about specific aspects and people connected to their work. They might take an extra moment to pray for each of them—offering gratitude, sending energy and hope, or just pondering their own connection to them. Take a moment yourself to ponder or pray for each learner, in turn, with whom you work. This would be time well used.

# CHAPTER 5

## Spirituality in the Workplace

In Chapters 3 and 4 we looked at how adult educators and trainers could integrate spirituality into their own lives and practices. Here we will talk about integrating a personal emphasis on spirituality into the workplace. There is growing interest in spirituality at work in many organizational settings where educators practice, such as colleges and universities, health care and social services, business and industry, and not-for-profit agencies. This interest appears related to higher stress, general malaise, and what Dirkx (2000) argues to be a "crisis of meaning" in the contemporary workplace. Dirkx explains that fundamentally we seek identity and purpose in our work:

> From a spiritual perspective, work expresses a particular relation of our selves to our work, and reflects a deep, inner capacity to see meaning in what one is doing and to approach one's work as an expression of one's inner self. Our work represents a "way of being," moving toward one's fullest participation in life, and contributing to the processes of individuation, self-actualization, and the potential for self-transcendence. Work as right work embodies self-expression, commitment, mindfulness, and conscious choice, and becomes an outward expression of our true inner selves. . . . It represents a kind of work that responds to an essential human need, to be a part of something larger than oneself, to feel connected with others to feel needed and valued. (p. 120)

In this chapter we describe some workplace pressures that may contribute to this perceived crisis, as well as some spiritual movements in work seeking to respond to the problem. These movements and programs are highly problematic for reasons we will explain throughout the chapter, which is one reason why we focus on ethics in considering ways to integrate spirituality in the workplace.

Our purpose is to move towards a vision of education within the workplace that is humane and that acknowledges both the relational dimension and the power dynamics of all workplace learning. The vision of generative work, while perhaps seen rarely, is not new. It has been offered by many writers concerned about how human individuals are affected by the naturalizing of productivity and efficiency, the division of labor, multi-tasking, and the hyperspeed of technological change. Feminist work theorist Hart (1992) suggests a vision of "sustenance work" whose ultimate purpose is to maintain and improve life, not produce commodities. Her vision is rooted in respectful, responsive relationships. Adult educator Welton (1991) argues that "the central challenge for adult educators is to develop a critical analytical and normative framework for understanding the constraints on and possibilities of developmental, learner-centered work" (p. 41).

> *The (former) Czech president, Vaclav Havel (1994), stated that the relativization of all moral norms, the crisis of authority, reduction of life to the pursuit of immediate material gain without regard for its general consequences — the very things Western democracy is most criticized for — does not originate in democracy but in that which modern man has lost: his transcendental anchor, and along with it the only genuine source of his responsibility and self-respect. It is because of this loss that democracy is losing much of its credibility.*

This authentic vision of education within the workplace moves towards the inclusion of human values, respect for human beings, and the integration of and recognition of spirituality, without subjugating these to the material gain of the organization and its elite. This is what Havel calls the transcendental anchor. Havel's vision is consistent with our own views about the possibilities for spirituality in workplace education.

As will become clear in this chapter, we do not advocate a "spiritual curriculum" in the workplace, nor do we believe that it is the place of the workplace educator to develop others' spirituality. However, we do encourage those educators interested in spirituality to pursue their own spiritual quest, to seek coherence between their spiritual insights and their daily living, and to embed their work with responsible spiritual practice. Educators can do much to suffuse the spaces and communities around them with invitation, compassion, and care—and a sense of anchor beyond productivity and material gain.

## THE CONTEMPORARY WORKPLACE

Given the vast differences in structure, mandate, culture, and activity of different sites, the term *workplace* may seem misleading and inadequate as a generic signifier attempting to embrace them all. However, cultural and sociological theorists of work describe characteristics and pressures shared among contemporary employing organizations. Barnett (1999) argues that global markets have created unprecedented competition among organizations, generating anxious focuses on continuous innovation, organizational change, and knowledge development. Sweeping change in workplace structures and values has supposedly spawned the "post-Fordist workplace" where, according to certain management enthusiasts, people work in self-directed teams rather than command-and-control hierarchies, their work motivated by meaning, mission, and values rather than incentives or fear, and the workplace is transformed from assembly lines of drudgery to empowering, creative communities of learning. However, as Solomon (1998) points out, the post-Fordist ideal hides much tension and struggle among employees for control of their own minds and souls, as well as their bodies and labor.

Meanwhile, as Foley (1999a) outlines, global overproduction and overcapacity have led to powerful corporate megalopolies controlling markets and currency—leading to increased privatization, deregulation of corporate movement and conduct, decreased social supports, mass casualization and temporization of workers, and increased workplace stress and violence. Large gaps are growing between the technical-professional-managerial elite of the industrial West, and subsistence workers in the global south and the West's "fourth world" of poverty and racialized, genderized margins. Meanwhile, amidst popular hype of today's workplace as a creative center for learning along with the concomitant push for workers' continuous training and development, Livingstone (1998) and others have shown mass underemployment: many workers' skills and knowledge already far exceed career opportunities and the employing organizations' ability to use them.

Flexibility is a dominant theme among descriptions of the contemporary workplace. Flexible workers (responsive, adaptive, transferable), flexible structures (insecure, fluid, adaptive to consumer demand and changing markets), flexible pay (increasingly contractual), and consequently flexible learning are assumed to ensure organizational competitiveness. Edwards (1998) and Garrick and Usher (1999) show the impacts on both a hidden curriculum of work and the individual subjectivities produced in workplaces where flexibility has become naturalized. Workers are expected to accept constant change as a given, to forego any expectation of stable employment and organizational loyalty, and to assume personal responsibility for adapting to organizations' changing needs for skills and labor. Workers' "learning" has become the legitimate foundation for organizational growth and survival, supposedly initiating a wide array of benefits for workers: personal development, meaningful relationships, creativity, even spiritual growth and happiness.

## EDUCATORS AND THE NEW WORKPLACE FOCUS ON SPIRIT

Amidst such bleak descriptions of today's workplace, energies of hope, renewal, and perhaps some opportunism are bubbling. Ethics codes and training are commanding serious attention in fields ranging from management to customer service, accounting, and engineering. Initiatives to promote employee wellness, including spiritual wellness, are proliferating. These include holistic training programs, experiments in changing work conditions to foster greater quality of life, and increased focus on reducing employee stress. Human resource development programs explicitly focused on encouraging employees' spiritual development abound. Leigh (1997) cites many U.S. programs with mandates such as "fostering social and spiritual transformation in the workplace. . . . dedicated to the further development of human consciousness through spiritual understanding" (p. 33).

According to popular management theory, business is becoming reinvented as a "community of souls" through shared values, love, trust, and respect. In the past decade, bestselling business titles have included *Jesus CEO: Using Ancient Wisdom for Visionary Leadership; The Stirring of Soul in the Workplace; and The Soul of a Business: Managing for Profit and the Common Good.* Secretan (1996), an HRD consultant to major corporations, shows in *Reclaiming Higher Ground: Creating Organizations that Inspire the Soul* that the way out of survival mode and into "true productivity" is through creating a spiritual "sanctuary" within the workplace. Books such as Secretan's mark the emergence of what Fenwick and Lange (1998) call "a new genre of HRD: merchant-missionaries who are busy marketing spirituality-based worker development programs to corporations" (p. 69).

Why has such a controversial and slippery topic emerged from the corporate closet? Bennis, in introducing a study of spirituality in organizations (Mitroff & Denton, 1999), asserts that "we're all on a quest for meaning and that the underlying cause of organizational dysfunction, ineffectiveness, and all manner of human stress is the lack of a spiritual foundation in the workplace" (p. xi). Imel (1998) found, in her literature review of spirituality in the workplace, the following reasons for growing focus on spirituality in work:

1. The growing number of corporate layoffs and the increase in downsizing. Workers are questioning the value of work and

seeking meaning and spirituality. When workers are under-valued by the organization to which they were loyal, questions about significance and the need for personal support increase.

2. The aging of the work force. As Baby Boomers age, their needs dominate the workplace. The Sixties' generation, who have been ubiquitously characterized as pursuing personal questions about life's meaning and spirituality, are negotiating mid- to late-career stages which are typified by increased reflection on the purpose of their work in the big picture.

3. The decline in traditional networks of support force people to question the location of meaning, hope, and inspiration for what they want to do in this world. Many of us are aware that relocation, family breakdowns, and the constant re-configurations of family structures have created a yearning for relational connection, and perhaps a search for alternate families.

4. Changes in organizational structure have created a work-place with less structure and more people-orientation. On the face of it, this "freedom" seems good. But it comes at a cost. For many people hierarchy provides an almost paternal comfort. They may moan, but to "know one's place" is re-laxing. Get rid of traditional structures, and this comfort dis-appears. The breakdown of organizational structures at least provides a fertile ground for discussions about personal con-cerns such as spirituality. These open-format organizations, sometimes characterized by fewer boundaries between man-agers and workers, also tend to promote closer working re-lationships among employees. The quality of talk changes as people become closer.

Although still in a beginning stage, research on spirituality in the workplace is growing though most is largely uncritical and positively biased towards spirituality. One of the more ex-tensive studies of spirituality in the workplace was Mitroff and Denton's (1999) *A Spiritual Audit of Corporate America: A*

*Hard Look at Spirituality, Religion, and Values in the Work-place.* These researchers and others such as Nadesan (1999) have argued that spirituality can help businesses become more humane, socially active, and environmentally responsible.

Mitroff and Denton (1999) interviewed 90 managers and executives, studied published literature on the topic of spirituality, and mailed a questionnaire to 2000 human resource managers and executives. They had a 100% success rate with the interviews and considerably less with the questionnaires (only 131 responses). Regardless of the low questionnaire response rate, the breadth of their interviews allows the findings of the study to stand as important. Their study helped them identify five different types of spiritually oriented organizations. The first type was the religiously based organization, usually oriented to the teachings of Christ and to furthering Christ's mission on earth. Mitroff and Denton found such organizations to be typically fundamentalist, where workers were expected to follow a code of working and living, and to be dedicated to the religious mission of the organization.

The second type of organization was the evolutionary organization, which often had moved from being religious to being spiritual. The YMCA, for instance, moved from being primarily Protestant to being more ecumenical. In fact, one YMCA chapter has a Jewish male director. This change in orientation was often connected with a values-based approach. The third type of organization was the recovering company, or one based on the principles of Alcoholics Anonymous. (Mitroff and Denton found no examples of this). The fourth type was the socially responsible organization, typified by Ben & Jerry's, the ice-cream retailer that supports environmentally sensitive projects. The fifth type of organization was the values-based organization. The philosophy of a values-based organization centers on the belief that personal values create ethical organizations. According to Mitroff and Denton, this was typified by a family-oriented organization that often used "family" language to describe itself and promoted the Golden Rule—do onto others as you would have them do unto you.

Along with identifying models of spiritual organizations, Mitroff and Denton's study found that respondents had similar definitions of spirituality: "Spirituality is the basic desire to find ultimate meaning and purpose in one's life and to live an integrated life" (p. xv). Their research showed that participants were not at all confused about what spirituality meant to them. They had a general understanding of its meaning, which challenges the academic idea that spirituality must be redefined in each situation in which it is used, if its meaning is to be understood. (See, for example, the discussion of the term in Chapter 1.)

Second, Mitroff and Denton found that the people interviewed wanted their lives to be wholly integrated, to be one, rather than separated into many parts. Participants saw spirituality as a lifelong quest, not an isolated part of their lives that could be appended or addressed during a weekend service. As a consequence, participants were interested in acknowledging their spirituality as an integral part of who they were.

A third finding was that participants made a separation between spirituality and religion. Religion was an inappropriate topic for workplace discussion, but discussing spirituality was fine. Participants wanted their lives acknowledged as holistic, but were concerned that their notions of spirituality and religion should remain separate. Although they hoped to have their spiritual dimension acknowledged at work, they were equally sure they did not want religion to become part of their workplace. The findings of this study raise questions about how to carefully separate religion from spirituality and how to draw a line between appropriate and inappropriate discussions.

A fourth finding was that those interviewed were interested in becoming familiar with models of how one might practice spirituality in the workplace, without offending others who might not hold similar values. Participants wanted to "nourish" their souls in nonreligious ways; but did not know how. Because they could not identify models for their desired behavior, they feared using words like *religion* and *spirituality* at work. Interestingly, most respondents were unable to cite examples of religiously based organizations other than Ben & Jerry's and the Body Shop.

From the organization's point of view, a sense of spirituality in the workplace disciplines employees to (a) be less fearful of their organizations, (b) be far less likely to compromise their basic beliefs and values in the workplace, (c) perceive their organization as significantly more profitable, and (d) report that they can bring significantly more of their complete selves to work, specifically their creativity and intelligence (Mitroff & Denton, 1999, p. xiv). McMillen (1993) explains that putting resources into spirituality can "produce" more fully developed workers, highly attuned to their identities, strengths, and weaknesses. Spiritual employees bring more energy, effort, and clarity to their jobs. Thus, issues of initiative, responsibility, motivation, commitment, and productivity supposedly resolve themselves. And, of course, as McMillen points out, health insurance costs, absenteeism, and enthusiasm help sell spiritual benefits.

> *In* A Day of Rest: Creating a Spiritual Space in Your Week, *Hickman (1999) suggests that we all need to restore a sanctuary in our hectic lives. Hickman makes one simple suggestion: honor a Sabbath, whether it is the Muslims' Friday, the Jews' Saturday, the Christians' Sunday, or a day of spiritual rest and renewal one chooses. . . . Focusing primarily on Jewish, Christian, and Islamic traditions, Hickman acknowledges that people can find spiritual moments of calm outside an institutional religious community. She suggests that the peacefulness of "Sabbath" can be brought to any day or any season of the year. It is interesting to note the root connection of "sabbath" to "sabbatical," a period of rest or study leave away from one's everyday work.*

What is frightening is an apparent seamless conflation of corporate purpose with these discourse and promises of spirituality. When people are encouraged to abandon rationality and open themselves to spiritual ways of knowing, their vulnerability is open to manipulation. "Spiritual" educators may unwittingly become soul harvesters serving the organization's bottom line. Many are themselves competitive businesses seeking a novel market niche, and they are apparently finding it as hawkers of the holy to corporate interest. One rather uncomfortable example is illustrated by Pacific Institute's "Purpose of Life" curriculum, offered to its Fortune 500 company clients by educators such as Catholic priest Father Bob Spitzer (Finlayson, 1997). This curriculum focuses on developing spiritual ethics and "happiness" among workers, "the happiness we feel from making a difference to someone or something beyond [ourselves]" (p. H4). Father Bob demonstrates how such happiness increases productivity, markets, return on investment, and long-term viability.

Work choices that are at bottom moral/ethical decisions are increasingly seen as technical decisions to increase productivity. When a "do more and faster" mentality predominates, both workers and management can become blind to how so many everyday work decisions of their workplaces are really ethical decisions—choices of the spiritual realm. For example, think of how often workers are faced with choosing actions that will protect their job but hurt a friend or contravene an ethical principle they value. Then think of how many people claim that the work they used to love—their vocations—have become stress-filled, devoid of creative expression, compromised in ethical integrity, and burdensome with paperwork and administrivia that seem constantly to get in the way of meaningful action. Think of processing e-mail, which for many office workers swallows more and more numbing chunks of time. And, how does e-mail reshape the personality of an interaction? How can one connect meaningfully with people through a medium which expects efficient, concise immediacy but distances people from each other? Our preoccupation with productivity overloads our days with tasks crowded into breathless timelines, leaving little time to connect with people through meaningful talk, to connect with our activities and environments through mindful engagement, or to connect with our own feelings, meanings, and bodies through reflection. Why do more and faster? What is truly being accomplished? These are questions of the spirit.

## MOVING TOWARDS ETHICAL INTEGRATION OF SPIRITUALITY AND WORK

If we renounce the promotion of organization-enhancing productivity as a legitimate purpose for educators to venture into the private realms of workers' spirituality, do we then avoid all mentions of the spiritual in the workplace for fear of being invasive? How do we as educators find ethical ways to enable more spirit-filled work, and reduce spirit-deadening conditions and activities, while avoiding repressive evangelism, exclusion, or manipulation?

We believe there are three ethical and defensible approaches to promoting spirituality in work. First is acknowledging, developing, and expressing one's own spirituality as an inherent part of one's practice as a workplace educator. Several approaches are offered in the following section describing different understandings of the spiritual journey and ways to enhance it.

Second is ensuring that the environment of one's practice as an educator is congruent with one's spiritual values and invites others, where appropriate, to express and explore their own integration of spirituality and work.

Third and perhaps most important is continual questioning of one's intentions and actions when invoking the spiritual in workplace education. We must ask, *For what purpose is spirituality being promoted in this workplace?* We maintain that the only defensible purpose is dedicated to creating a more compassionate life-giving workspace that enables people to find fulfillment and personal meaning in their work and that nurtures connectedness and caring.

> *One influential work on the Sabbath is Abraham Heschel's 1951 book of the same name. In* The Sabbath, *Heschel tells the story of "Rabbi Loew of Prague (died 1609) [who] was called 'Tall Rabbi Loew' because on the Sabbath he looked a head taller than during the six days of the week" (p. 88). This special blessing on holy people underscores the importance of rest on the Sabbath with the Jewish tradition.*

## PROMOTING SPIRITUALITY IN THE LIFE
## OF THE WORKPLACE EDUCATOR

J. A. Neal (1997) has developed five guidelines for teaching management education from a spiritual perspective. These
guidelines begin with "knowing thyself." Truly and intimately
knowing oneself is the basis for all further spiritual development.
Self-awareness starts with questioning yourself as a teacher,
looking at what you do, and asking why you do it. Explaining
how she uses this guideline in her own teaching, Neal says that
she tries to stretch herself by trying new ways of teaching and
learning in every new situation. She believes this results in more
personal energy as an educator, more awareness, and more attentiveness to students. This approach is catching. Once adopted
by the teacher, it can then be shared with students. A result is
that students gain increased opportunities to challenge themselves to become more self-aware.

Neal's second guideline for workplace educators is to act
with authenticity and congruence in all aspects of one's practice.
Neal advocates being true to yourself, being real, and being vulnerable. Neal acknowledges that the type of openness she asks
for can be difficult even for the best educators. She notes one
specific approach is to create a classroom climate where students
feel free to state their views and feelings and to offer feedback
about how things are going in the class.

The third guideline Neal advocates for integrating spirituality into the life of the educator is to honor the beliefs of others.
Such respect begins with a discussion of your own spirituality
in the classroom, a practice that she follows. She acknowledges
that this practice might seem dangerous for some, but notes that
a climate of trust and honesty can minimize the problem. She
acknowledges also that, while her views about spirituality are
her views, others may have different views. Neal uses values
assessments that challenge students to consider their own values, their assumptions, and the ways they enact what they believe.

The fourth guideline Neal recommends is to be as trusting

as possible. This means believing learners will do what they say they will do, and ensuring that you do what you say you will do.

Finally, Neal recommends that educators maintain their own spiritual practice. Her research with those who try to integrate spirituality into their workplace shows that many spend time with nature as their spiritual practice. Others meditate or pray daily. Neal makes her spiritual disciplines part of her daily routine and tries to follow them regularly. Neal admits that when she does not follow them, she notices a decline in her ability to handle stress and pressure.

The overall emphasis is not upon developing others' spirituality, but focusing upon one's own. As one seeks to become attuned to the personal spiritual life, one becomes aware of the incongruences between one's spirituality, daily activity, and environment. As Thomas Moore (1994) explains in *Care of the Soul*, one begins listening to personal pain, fear, joy, and needs as the voice of the soul. Such attunement begins affecting how, as an educator, one listens and responds to others, an influence which begins to suffuse relationships with a new and difficult-to-name quality. One also begins to notice and hopefully try to change elements of everyday work that impede one's own spiritual growth as an educator or harm the spirit. This is how we believe an educator infuses the workplace with spirituality—ethically and non-manipulatively.

We believe different representations of the spiritual journey are helpful in this process, to assist those pursuing a spiritual journey in their discernment. In the following section, four depictions of the developing spiritual life are offered for the personal meditation of educators.

> *Truth is housed in numerous places. Some of the female adult educators whom Tisdell (1999b) interviewed indicated that they embrace a number of religious traditions and practices, all at once. One study participant, Shirley, was raised Christian but now does not belong to a church. She meditates daily, centering on the mantra "God is love." Her purpose in life "is to restore and maintain the balance, which is, order, justice . . . and truth. My intention is*

*to walk my convictions . . . trying to bring forth the power of God in myself. When people ask I say I'm Muslim because the Muslim is one who submits to the will of God." (pp. 3–4)*

## DEPICTIONS OF THE SPIRITUAL JOURNEY

Several authors have attempted to address the issue of the spiritual journey and provide a path or map of the spiritual life others might follow. Here, we identify four of these maps (Elkins, Hedstrom, Hughes, Leaf, & Saunders, 1988; Fowler, 1981; Neal, 2000b; Tisdell, 2000b). As we write about these maps, we will highlight key points of interest and comment on them. We challenge readers to consider how their own spiritual journeys compare with the maps outlined here. If they do not, we encourage asking questions about what aids or prevents the growth of spiritual life within the workplace.

*Feminist educator bell hooks (1999) writes that "one of the things that we must do as teachers is twirl around and around, and find out what works with the situation that we're in. Our models might not work. And that twirling, changing, is part of the empowerment." (p. 128)*

### The Spiritual Journey as Life Phases

In a *Spiritatwork* article called "Spiritual Evolution," J. A. Neal (2000b) discusses the results of her study in a facilitated online discussion group. Over a three-year period, Neal dialogued with 150 people, had over 700 informal conversations, and carried out approximately 40 in-depth interviews about spirituality in the workplace. The interest in spirituality came from employees in a variety of economic sectors, including nonprofit, for profit, governmental, and religious organizations. However, Neal noted that most interest in the topic came from people in careers such as consulting, education, and healthcare.

From her study, Neal identified a progression she believes typifies the spiritual journey of most participants.

- Segmentation. In this phase, people separate or compartmentalize the various parts of their lives, keeping home, spirituality, and relationships separate from work. People tend to resist connecting these parts and refuse to make "what happens on Sunday connect to what happens on Monday." Although they may be part of a religious or spiritual organization such as a church or mosque, people in this phase are likely to keep these parts of their life separate.
- Crisis of some sort. For many people, a life event forces them to see the world in a new way and challenges them to look at where they have come from and where they are going. This crisis might be a layoff at work, the death of a close friend or relative, or a serious illness. This phase is usually accompanied by fear and unknowing.
- Dark night of the soul. In this phase, people search for answers. They often rediscover spirituality and may even return to the religion they grew up with. They are unsure about what to do and where to go. As a result, they feel down and out.
- Right livelihood. In this phase, people report moments of grace in their lives. This phase might include significant life changes such as a new job or new practices.
- Beneficial presence. Now people further refocus their energy. Perhaps this involves a break from work, or a positive, learning time in their own spiritual lives.

## The Spiritual Journey as Progressive Stages

Other models of spirituality exist which further address issues such as those J. A. Neal (2000b) has raised. One of the most popular was developed by Fowler (1981) in *Stages of Faith*. Although Fowler uses the language of religion (e.g., faith), he defines faith broadly, closer to a typical definition of spirituality.

- Stage 1, intuitive projective faith, occurs from ages 2–6. In this stage, the child sees the world through an imaginative and creative lens. This stage is unrestrained by logic and is typified by the child's belief in magic and that all things are possible to one who believes.

- Stage 2, mythical-literal faith, lasts until adolescence. In this stage, the child sees things as they are in their concrete sense. Faith is literal and might include a narrative family of ritual and myth.
- Stage 3, synthetic-conventional faith, lasts from teenage years to early adulthood. This stage is characterized by affinity or conformity with the peer group. Whatever the group believes to be true, the teen will also believe.
- Stage 4, individuating-reflexive faith, lasts from early adulthood to beyond. In this stage, adults develop a more critical questioning attitude to the faith traditions they have been handed about religion and spirituality. This questioning may result in anger or disappointment at the many paradoxes and polarities that confound faith and life.
- Stage 5, conjunctive faith, occurs during a person's midlife or later. Rules and regulations no longer bind this stage. People deal more seriously with what suppressed or prevented them from being independent in the last stage. They may return to sacred symbol, story, tradition, liturgy, and spiritual community. However, these moves are made on their own terms and do not necessarily coincide with those of an organization.
- Stage 6, universalizing faith, is rarely achieved. In this stage, humans feel at one with all of humanity and are committed to universal issues of love, peace, and justice.

Fowler (1981) notes that literature abounds with examples of individuals who struggle through these stages. Examples include Dostoevsky's Alyosha, who makes a breakthrough when he recovers his religion, and Joyce's Stephen Dedalus, who finally rejects his religious upbringing. What seems apparent to us is how life has changed in the 20 years since Fowler created his stages. Today, perhaps Fowler's categories could best be represented as a circle—where Stage 6 loops back to a naïve, almost pre-thoughtful stage where "universal" beliefs seem mashed together as if they lacked any differences at all—a stage more understood for chanting and slogans than commitment.

## The Spiritual Journey as Spirals

The third map, surveyed by Tisdell (2000b), includes a feminist, social justice perspective. This map is drawn from her qualitative research with 16 women of diverse cultural, social, and ethnic backgrounds, all of whom are social activists. Rather than a linear progression of phases or even a series of stages, Tisdell found that the women, all of whom had been raised in a religious tradition, spiraled away from, back to, and away from their religious traditions. Although her participants may have rejected the sexism, racism, and hypocrisy of their religious tradition, they often reclaimed symbols and metaphors of the tradition that held meaning for them.

Tisdell cites the example of a woman who had moved away from Roman Catholicism but still found symbolic meaning in the Resurrection. In contrast to Fowler's highly rational model, these women experienced symbols and images in ways that were sometimes beyond language. Tisdell does not impose a series of stages or phases on what she describes as this spiraling effect. Her depiction serves as a challenge to more linear progressions that are easier to categorize but may substitute form for accuracy.

## The Spiritual Journey as Developing Awareness

A study by Elkins et al. (1988) examined spiritual lives and concluded that spirituality develops through clusters of experiences that increase awareness of numinous dimensions in life. Nine dimensions were identified:

1. Transcendent dimension, an awareness of some higher power or nonrational, connective and unseen dimension extending beyond the individual consciousness.

2. Meaning and purpose in life, an experience of a personal quest.

3. Mission in life, an awareness of a personally important vocation that is one's responsibility to fulfill.

4. The sacred, an awareness of its embeddedness in all things and all life, and inspiring daily awe and wonder.

5. Material values appreciated in practical perspective with the nonmaterial.

6. Altruism, an awareness of others' needs and the stirrings of compassion within.

7. Idealism, a growing sense of the possibilities for bettering one's own sphere of the world.

8. The tragic, an awareness of human pain, suffering, and death.

9. Fruits of spirituality, an awareness of one's changing relationships with self, others, nature, life, and the transcendent.

## Comparisons and Contrasts

Each of these four maps of the spiritual life challenges our personal experiences in some way. For instance, the notion that to be spiritual one must first encounter a crisis, seemingly the basis of J. A. Neal's (2000b) stage theory, can be challenged by those whose spiritual journey has grown naturally through their childhood. For example, Coles's (1990) extensive work *The Spiritual Life of Children* attests to the strong and creative spiritual lives many children have and which many can identify with. Similarly, Fowler's (1981) model challenges those who disagree that to be spiritually mature one must go through a phase of breaking with the rules and traditions of organized religion. Fowler's use of a Judeo-Christian population for his study (97% of all his study participants), and his lack of attention to the sociocultural context and construction of his stages of faith, challenge those who want a more inclusive way of mapping the spiritual journey.

Tisdell's (2000b) spirals challenge those who need a clearer, more comprehensive view of the spiritual life over the lifespan and not a snapshot in time. Elkins et al. (1988) outlines openings offered by different areas of human experience for developing awareness of spiritual dimensions in life. These challenges aside, all four maps of the spiritual journey help provide entrée to the spiritual world and help us examine or remember the critical events in our spiritual journeys. A greater truth, perhaps, is that these models show that many conceive their spiritual life as a journey. The spiritual lives of most people are filled with twists and turns, periods of confusion as well as clarity. A single human experience rarely includes all the experiences and intensity (or lack of intensity) which phase and stage theories suggest. One life differs from another, and the impact of the same event differs from human to human. Hence, while metaphors such as journey, spiral, travel, and map may be helpful, every spiritual life is different and needs to explore its own metaphors to make sense of the questions and experiences. Vogel (2000) explains that, "As we reckon with our spiritual lives, we encounter, reflect, imagine, and create different ways of seeing and engaging persons and situations with renewed energy, hope, and vision" (p. 18).

> *The great 16th-century mystic and chronicler of her spiritual life, Teresa of Avila (1946), was 40 years old before her first deep spiritual experience. Her spirituality was a complex mix of political activity, rich and rewarding relationships with men and women, prayerful meditation, and intense reform initiatives in the Carmelite monastic order. Knowing our own journey and studying the work of others such as Teresa, who have dedicated their entire lives to exploring their spiritual journey, can be helpful for those adult educators and trainers interested in spirituality. In her book* The Interior Castle, *Teresa compares her soul to a castle that has many rooms, just as heaven is a mansion of many rooms. Teresa's mystical visions and rich prayer life became the impetus for her major reform movement, in which she brought the Carmelite order back to its early focus on simplicity and caring for the poor. Her reform led her into many political battles with the hierarchy and even with her own sisters. She was an institutional rebel in every*

*sense and clearly dispelled the notion of a quiet, retiring, solitary woman religious. Hers was the spirituality of the world.*

## STARTING POINTS FOR FURTHER REFLECTION

1. Try drawing a map of your spiritual journey. Use signposts and any other markers or metaphors you think appropriate to indicate the significant points on your journey.

2. Does your spiritual life resemble any of those by J. A. Neal, Fowler, Elkins et al., or Tisdell? What is your own symbol for the journey?

3. Try drawing a map of your organization's spiritual journey. Answer questions 1 and 2 above, with the organization in mind.

## INTEGRATING SPIRITUALITY WITH THE WORKPLACE ENVIRONMENT

According to Ionnone and Obenauf (1999), environments that promote spirituality through learning are characterized by "flexibility, creativity, newness, engagement, reflectiveness, and teacher and student stories of meaning-making are honored" (p. 739). For workplace educators, an environment is not only physical structures and tools, but also a series of communities and relationships involving culture and language. All aspects of our practice, whether negotiating a new program with colleagues, working with a contractor to write educational materials, conducting needs assessments of staff, justifying the funds for an employee resource center, or facilitating educational programs for workers, become the environments we create through our interactions with others. As explained above, we cannot help influencing these environments when we seek personal spiritual growth and congruence between our own spirituality and our work as educators.

Dirkx (2000) argues that despite the increasing interest in spirituality at work and the concurrent critique of "work spirituality" programs, in most organizations there is little real acknowledgement or integration of spirituality in work. Dirkx suggests that the growing "spirituality of work" movement is a fundamental expression of soul grieving the loss of meaning in work, and yearning for a connection to something (the divine? the sacred? the soul?) which may lift us from malaise. Dirkx describes a vision of work and the organization "through soul," where earthly being and work are embraced "as a kind of prayer in itself" (p. 122). When we infuse our everyday material work activities, however dirty or mundane, with spiritual practice, we stop the split of our labor and our whole, connection-seeking, meaning-starved spirits. We reconnect the isolated interior life with the busy exterior life of work. We may rediscover opportunities for creative discovery and expression, communion with others, and meaning—not necessarily in grandiose transcendent experiences but in the small beauties of everyday moments.

Glazer (1999) describes sacredness in everyday activity as:

> growing out of two basic quantities of our experience: awareness and wholeness. Awareness is a natural, self-manifesting quality: it is our ability to perceive, experience and know. A sense of awareness can be cultivated (or enhanced) through mindfulness or attentiveness. The development of awareness enables us to bring a greater and greater sense of presence to the repercussions and meaning of our lives.
>
> Wholeness is the inherent, seamless, interdependent quality of the world. Wholeness, indeed, is the fact of the matter: the things of the world (including us) are already connected, are already in relationship, are already in union. Wholeness, however, can be cultivated within us by experiencing this nondual quality of the world. Through experiences of awareness and wholeness, we begin to establish the view of the sacred. (p. 10)

Fox (1983) similarly urges spiritual healing of work and work environments through the restoration of balanced and mutual relationships. For him, this begins with the personal spiritual journey as detaching from endless striving and worldly desire. When one becomes open to pain, suffering, anguish, and the fear within oneself, one hears the pain of others. Pain links humans to each other, for pain is schooling in compassion (pp. 143, 145). Compassion for other people helps blur destructive boundaries of identity, possession, and authority. Fox, Dirkx (2000), and others also focus on the yearning for creative expression in work as a spiritual need. Opportunities for creativity can be provided through workers' assignment to new creative teams, involvement in new large or small projects, or opportunities to redesign a work process or one's own job responsibilities. Much has been written about the need for such opportunities to be meaningful and appropriate to individual workers' own requests, and to be provided equitably, with suitable support and resources (Billett, 2001). The common link among these writings is the avoidance of offering practical strategies to "spiritualize" environments. We do not believe that the crisis of meaning in the workplace is healed through candle-lit workshops, meditational posters, or special praying rooms—although such additions to a workplace may certainly be appreciated by particular individuals pursuing their own spiritual journeys, and send messages about the organization's apparent commitment to acknowledging spirituality's importance. Similarly pleasant physical environments or attention to symbols, light, music, and space may soothe stress and promote physical comfort and energy, but they are not necessarily linked to spirituality. Or, the Internet may even provide some of the space that we are thinking of. For instance, the Dublin Jesuits (Elwood, 2000) opened a prayer space on the Internet where people can go to pray at various times in the day (http://www.sacredspace.ie/). This web space has prayers, reflections, and scripture readings that take about 10 minutes at the computer terminal to complete. This activity may indeed be one way an organization may allow its members to seek their own spiritual refreshment. We encourage emphasis on exploring one's own spiritual vocation as an educator, turning especially to extending one's spiritual practices in all of one's relationships and interactions. We believe that this deliberate attention to personal spirituality enables spirit-filled work environments.

## ETHICS AND SPIRITUALITY IN
## WORKPLACE EDUCATION

There are many ethical questions to be asked about integrating spirituality into workplace education. As adult educators and trainers, we need to prepare for the questions and be ready to help our co-learners understand and form their own questions.

The educator's role is defended by Socrates (495–405 BCE), who said, "The ideal condition / Would be, I admit, that men should be right by instinct / But since we are all likely to go astray / The reasonable thing is to learn from those who can teach." As adult educators and trainers, the first ethical question we must ask is whether it is even ethical to discuss spirituality in the workplace or to combine spirituality with workplace education. In the words of management writer Nadesan (1999): Should the corporation save your soul? Is it ethical to debate an issue that is so personal? These questions are the first many ask when starting to explore the place of spirituality in education and training.

Lawler's (2000) recent examination of the ethical dimensions of continuing professional education, for instance, raises specific issues for adult educators and trainers who plan educational programs for professionals within a structured organization. When introducing spirituality into education, there is always a potential conflict when the organization's vision (e.g., religious orientation, focus on servant leadership, exclusivity, lack of tolerance for differences) conflicts with the educator's vision of what is ethical and right. The educator must decide whether the right course of action is to challenge organizational leaders, refuse to be part of the proposed plan to implement the vision, leave the organization, or even act as whistle-blower. Most adult educators and trainers encounter ethical dilemmas that affect how they carry out programs and plans. However, when it comes to spirituality the issues are amplified because the topic is personal and difficult to separate from other individually held views. Therefore, it is imperative that adult educators and trainers seriously consider these questions in light of their own selves: What are our assumptions? What do we believe about spirituality? Where are potential conflicts for us? How can we prepare ourselves to negotiate the conflict?

The hypothetical cases below are based on potential ethical conflicts. We encourage you to put yourself into each situation and consider how you might deal with it.

## Case 1

Young-lee Kim, a corporate trainer, has been asked by the vice-president of training and development to design a program for his employer, an auto parts manufacturing company, that will help hourly waged employees realize their "full potential." The program is to be based on Stephen Covey's books advocating a specific values-based system of living. Although the program appears to present helpful principles, he is skeptical about the overtly spiritual nature of the material and examples, and the imposition of a single perspective on the personal lives of masses of workers. He also suspects company support has more to do with maximizing employees' productivity than with self-actualization of the employee. He debates how he can be involved and yet remain faithful to the organization and the employees. What possible courses of action might he follow?

## Case 2

Susan Power is a faculty development coordinator at a small Catholic college in the southern United States. She has been asked to serve as a liaison with the chaplain at the university and to work towards building a spirituality of justice among faculty so they will be more supportive of the service learning program the college administration recently started. Her job is to design educational sessions for departmental faculty meetings that help bring the faculty on side. She encounters resistance in every department. She knows that the university notoriously underpays faculty and has a record of discrimination. It is a matter of public record that the university has fired a female staff member who is lesbian. How might you handle this situation?

## Case 3

Rasa Kazan works for a large international development agency with no religious or spiritual ties. He understands from the participants in his predeparture programs that a strong spiritual dimension has led to their decisions to volunteer to go overseas. Some participants have been brought up in religious homes; others have had long involvement with organizations with strong social justice orientations. He wonders why the organizers resist addressing the issue of motivation, particularly spirituality, with participants. He is aware that the mission statement of the organization actually says that you cannot discuss religion, yet he decides to. Why do you suppose the organization is so opposed?

In thinking through these scenarios, Brockett's (1990) six ethical principles to guide educators' practice may be helpful:

1. Respect for learners

2. Justice in working with learners

3. Observation and integration of the rights and responsibilities of the learners

4. An attempt to maximize positive outcomes

5. Care for learners

6. A willingness to be self-reflective about one's own practice

Applied to the issue of spirituality, these principles highlight the needs of the learner and bring attention to the constant care and vigilance that are part of the work of education and training.

> *Meister Eckhart (1994), a Dominican priest who lived in the 13th century, made many observations on the balance of action and prayer. He once noted that "when we find ourselves under pressure or constraint, it will be apparent that we are more worked than working. . . . It is not that we should abandon, neglect or deny our inner self, but we should learn to work precisely in it, with in and from it in such a way that interiority turns into effective action and*

*effective action leads back to interiority and we become used to acting without any compulsion. For we should concentrate on this inner prompting, and act from it, whether through reading or prayer or—if it is fitting—some form of external activity. Though if the external activity destroys the internal one, we should give priority to the latter. But if both are united as one, then that is best for cooperating with God." (p. 45)*

## QUESTIONING SPIRITUALITY IN THE WORKPLACE

Ultimately, perhaps the most important question to confront when considering the integration of spirituality and work is whether this objective simply advances the encroachment of work and enterprise on important spaces of a worker's family, community, religion, friendships, and private contemplative life. Search for meaning and purpose, connectedness, transcendence, and other dimensions of spirituality traditionally unfold in these other spheres, away from the workplace. Is it desirable to incorporate all of the deepest human yearnings into work? Fenwick and Lange (1998) critique the problem when the search for meaning is taken over by the workplace in a "bid for market share of souls" (p. 65). Pointing out that human resource departments are offering care and support, they remind us that the motive is first to improve the organization's bottom line. Yet, the offer by the organization is typically tempting: "authentic community, holistic living, the meaning of life, personal healing, and purposeful action in a needy world" (p. 65).

Fenwick and Lange's (1998) critique of human resource development (HRD) and spirituality highlights several problems: First is the contradiction between authentic spirituality and HRD. One has a creative, energetic source; the other is profit driven. Second is the "fundamentalist" aspect to workplace spirituality. There is little room for diversity or "community, critical reflection, shared vision, and continuous innovation" (p. 75). Third is the problem with the invasion of HRD into the personal and spiritual dimension of one's life. Fourth is the belief that workers should surrender without discernment— the expected uncritical acceptance of the topic and its place in the workplace. Fenwick and Lange suggest a grounded rethinking of work, learning, and spirituality. They also suggest asking two questions of the organization: Whose interests are served? and Is the company trying to colonize the spirituality of the worker? Their work encourages a careful examination of motives and the willingness to err on the side of the workers.

Here we apply Fenwick and Lange's concerns to raise political and interpretive questions about the motives and interests of the organizational initiative to integrate spirituality into the workplace.

## Case 1

Tom Franck is the CEO of a medium-size manufacturing company in a large urban area in the American midwest. Tom spent the first 25 years of ownership of this company trying to build the quality of his products, marketing internationally, and making money for shareholders. Tom is a self-made man, who gives to his church and community, goes to work, fights unions, makes money, and devotes his life to capitalism.

At the age of 53 Tom's world changed when his 21-year-old son, a senior in college, was killed in a drunk-driving accident. This event caused Tom to fall apart. In his quest to find sense some meaning in his world, Tom turned to fundamentalist religion. Tom's new agenda is to share his new joy, pleasure, and solace in religion with his employees. He has directed his HRD department to begin integrating a spirituality dimension to employee training and education, and for the company to promote inspirational reading and prayer at work. Hourly employees are concerned. Their once secure jobs are now seemingly intertwined with an acceptance of this new religious drive.

## Case 2

Roger Thoms is the workplace educator for a local pulp and paper mill in a rural west coast town in the United States. This company has flexible workplace education program that in-

tegrates a number of human potential programs into the sched-
ule. The educational program involves about 60% of human development work in the programs, allowing employees to use
learning contracts to design how they want to do their learning
this year. More importantly, the company has a policy of environmental responsibility that keeps it accountable to the local
town and to the residents and limits resource use. This company
has had good worker programs and benefits for 30 years.

**Case 3**

Health care workers in a major urban children's hospital
have been called once again to an ethics training workshop.
Those who attend this workshop receive credit for completing
6 hours of CPE, which works towards the total required for
licensure. Health care workers must attend the workshops, but
basically all they hear at these sessions is "respect the patient's
wishes." They would like to hear more informed discourse from
researchers who have thought about the issues in a more complex way and who can help them examine their own problems
and beliefs. They know from the popular media that patients
with strong religious beliefs seem able to accept illness more
readily and tend to get well quicker. They would like their CPE
to address these connections, but hospital policy precludes these
conversations in educational sessions.

---

## STARTING POINTS FOR FURTHER REFLECTION

### Questions for Cases 1 and 2

1. What is the real intent of the workplace drive to spirituality?

2. Whose interests are served?

3. Whose conception of need drives the program, according to
   whose perception and whose authority?

4. Is the organization's design targeting the individual's spiritual needs as a final frontier of human capital?

5. Are the organizational policies consistent with the sudden emphasis on employee spirituality (inclusivity, family needs, stress)?

---

## STARTING POINTS FOR FURTHER REFLECTION

### Issuing Challenges to the Workplace

Based on their U.S. study of those who contributed to the common good, Daloz et al. (1996) found that 75% of the men and women identified religious or spiritual influences in their life that motivated them to work for the common good. These findings were not job-specific and were consistent across business, the arts, and health care. Focusing directly on business, Daloz et al. assert that the business community has untold opportunities to support the global commons. Based on extensive interviews, the research identified ways that business is working towards the common good.

Assess each of these findings and ask: Is this view possible in my workplace? If it is not, what limits it?

- "Assess the strengths and limits of an ideology of individualism and market logic" (p. 234).
- "[Build] a workplace characterized by respect for difference and commitment to the well-being of all" (p. 234).
- "Support commitments to the common good" (p. 235).

---

## SUMMARY

How, in fact, workplace educators can address spirituality in their work is a question that obviously challenges us for an answer. We have argued here that one approach for educators concerned about spirituality is to attend to their own spiritual development and to the integration of their spirituality into the way they live their own practice. This integration does not necessarily require incorporating explicit discussion of spirituality into conversations and educational materials, although for some like J. A. Neal (1997), it might. For others it is more a matter of living personal spiritual beliefs, whatever they may be. Many of the spiritual authors appear to share beliefs in connectedness and compassion for people, reverence for all living things, and the potential sacredness of each task and moment in one's work life.

This chapter has also shown the darker potential for oppression, manipulation, and exclusion in presenting spiritual programs in the workplace. Even when these are aimed at improving workers' morale and well-being, many tend to target employees as requiring "fixing" through spiritual development. Not only does this render systemic problems to be the responsibility of individual workers, but it subjugates individual spirituality under the authority of the employer—who wields the enormous power of a paycheck. But rather than ban spirituality from organizations, we have suggested that tolerance and understanding, and even careful encouragement, of individual spiritual expression in work might be an acceptable approach. When doing so, however, we must be highly sensitive to the development of any dominant norms that can impose subtle forms of exclusion or discrimination These and other difficult ethical issues surrounding spirituality and work deserve to be pondered at length, especially given the implications for the quality of the work environment and the needs of the worker.

Perhaps the most important spiritual task facing educators involves clear-eyed discernment of their own and their organization's intentions for the role of spirituality in workplace education. We must continually ask ourselves, *For what purpose is spirituality being promoted in this workplace?* The only defensible purposes are those which are ultimately congruent with our own deepest spiritual beliefs about our vocation as educators.

# CHAPTER 6

## Adult Educators and Trainers as Leaders of Change

This chapter concludes our discussion of spirituality. We will attempt to show how the acknowledgment and integration of spirituality can help the field of adult education and training reach the fullness of its founders' vision. Part of the rich tradition of this field, and frankly the pride we share in working in the area, is that throughout its history, practitioners and researchers struggled for the common good, for community improvement, and often for the underdog. This tradition inspires us. It seems especially to stand in stark contrast to what we seen in the academic landscape of our contemporary world. As we noted earlier, we lament what we see as a tendency to celebrate the negative and the increasing push of educators and scholars towards esoteric self-interest and self-absorption that seems often to minimize the huge needs so apparent to us as we look over the human geography of the world we live in.

As we attempt to bring the book's main argument to closure, we will emphasize vision and purpose. Without vision and purpose, we believe that spirituality in our discipline is lost. We believe the need for greater vision is fundamental to adult education and training, and is at least one reason for making the study of spirituality increasingly significant in all areas of our field.

We also believe that when people ask for bread, we should not give them stones. Our learners are demanding support for their spiritual needs, and we believe that as educators and trainers we are compelled to consider, to attend, and to help them on their own spiritual growth. We believe that the curriculum of almost every hero of adult education and training we have known has been to establish, within the groups they worked with, a vision of success and possibility.

Finally, we believe that clear thinking and grounded action are required to understand and integrate spirituality into practice in ethical and meaningful ways. In this chapter, we suggest some resources and further reading that we believe might help our colleagues on their spiritual journey.

In Chapter 1, we made much ado about the historical basis for the integration of spirituality into adult education and training. Since we started this book, one thing has become very clear. The interest in spirituality in workplace education is not only historical but has strong support and commitment from a variety of our colleagues, many of whom travel with us on a spiritual journey. Both our research and our daily conversations and e-mails from these colleagues are sharings of their travels, their luggage, and their weariness and joy as they work out the place of spirituality in their lives. We also admit that reading and writing about spirituality have given us a more finely attuned sense of the sacred in our everyday world. We have come to believe that there are worlds and possibilities that we have not even yet begun to explore.

As we complete this book, some of the many changes in our own field have become obvious to us. Things have changed since the early days of adult education and training. For instance, we no longer celebrate our heroes—in fact, we seem eager to critique them, forgetting how difficult their work and the gaining of their unique visions must have been. For example, we often hear our colleagues minimize the work of the visionary Malcolm Knowles, whose far-reaching and comprehensive account, *The Adult Education Movement in the United States* (1962), named religious organizations as significant and distinct providers of adult education. Not only do we seem to be ashamed of Knowles's work, we are certain that no one needs to be told that pride of place no longer exists. But, our work has not disheartened us. What does exist in adult education and training is exciting to us. The possibilities of reclaiming and extending the field are great. We see this field as an area of turmoil, and often without focus. But, this does not mean that there are not localized pockets of miracles.

For example, some of the interests in spirituality and meaning making have become less centralized in organized groups, and are now being addressed by practitioners and researchers in many different settings. These settings include continuing professional education, nursing education, and workplace education. In fact, many philanthropic organizations have given resources to furthering the cause. These include the Pew, Lilly, and Fetzer foundations, which provide support for the integration of spirituality into education.

Even the interests of our own universities have grown in area in the spiritual. The Department of Secondary Education at the University of Alberta, for example, presently has almost 20 graduate students specifically studying curriculum in religious and moral education. Even 15 years ago, there were few programs outside religious institutions. And, within Canada, a conference of Christian religious educators titled "With Heart and Mind" meets every second year. Its express purpose is to foster dialogue between Christians within religious-based educational institutions and secular institutions. These conferences also include colleagues from the United States. Such activities are encouraging.

> *Often we do not have the eyes to see what is around us. Brazilian popular educator Augusto Boal (1998) points out that seeing is a challenge for most of us: "Looking is a biological act; open eyes look. Seeing is an act of conscience." (p. 79)*

## ADULT EDUCATORS AND TRAINERS AS LEADERS OF CHANGE

If you are an adult educator or trainer who wishes to attend to spirituality within your work, your challenge is great. Certainly, there is interest; however, the dissemination and distribution of this interest will likely be difficult. It's a tricky thing to incorporate spirituality well and with respect. Workplace educators, for instance, are called to attend to the spirit in their work. They are challenged to develop their own spirituality and to help develop the spirituality of others. Think about this statement. Adult educators and trainers have the potential to affect not only how workplace education is carried out in the present, but also how the workplace unfolds in the future. This is why we believe that adult educators and trainers exercise great power in at least two areas—how they educate and how the organization develops.

In *Spirited Leading and Learning: Process Wisdom for a New Age,* Peter Vaill (1998) strongly supports the potential of adult educators and trainers to effect a paradigm shift. Extended to spirituality, educators indeed have the opportunity to influence how spirituality is integrated, responded to, and how it affects the employees. We hope our book is part of this continuing activity, but it is only one part. Vaill points out that adult education and trainers need to provide leadership for change. Speaking from his extensive experience as a teacher of adults, he asserts that educators (though he seems to refer mainly to those who work in higher education) can provide this leadership in a number of ways. He builds on Kuhn's (1970) concept of paradigm shift, and the four broad elements Kuhn assigned to each discipline's matrix (paradigm):

1. Symbolic generalizations, or the basic assumptions about how the paradigm works

2. Metaphysical assumptions, or what people believe to be the real parts of the paradigm

3. Values, or the priorities, meanings and directions of the paradigm

4. Exemplars, or the examples that embody the best of the paradigm

Following Vaill (1998), we can apply Kuhn's four elements to illustrate how researchers and practitioners can be part of a paradigm shift that impacts thinking about spirituality and adult education and training. According to Kuhn, those who create new paradigms are often new to the field and able to see alternative ways of seeing and doing their work, and of contributing to the field. In some ways, we are all new to the field—because the integration of spirituality in adult education and training is a new juxtaposition of disciplines.

If our book does nothing else, we hope it challenges adult educators and trainers to think about the existing paradigm in the field. We hope it helps adult educators address how spirituality has been given to and received by them, and how our research and practice can be improved. We hope that the discussion of spirituality becomes a full and integral dimension of our own field of adult education and training. Finally, we challenge our readers to think of the existing paradigm of adult education and training—as they know it—and to consider how this paradigm might be configured differently.

> *Thirteenth-century mystic Julian of Norwich (1978) cultivated her own ways of seeing God in the world. Here is what she saw in her hand: "And in this [the Lord] showed me something small, no bigger than a hazelnut, lying in the palm of my hand, as it seemed to me, and it was as round as a ball. I looked at it with my eye of understanding and thought: What can this be?.... In this little thing I saw three properties. The first is that God made it, the second is that God loves it, the third is that God preserves it." (p. 183)*

## Paradigm Shift in Adult Education and Training

Here are Kuhn's (1970) four elements of a paradigm and how they might interact to create a paradigm shift.

*Symbolic generalizations* refer to how things are supposed to work or operate within a discipline. These "givens" make work in adult education and training possible. Symbolic generalizations refer to commonly accepted generalizations about how things are. For example, adult education and training are all too often based on a mechanistic vision of communicating knowledge and skills to participants. Adult education and training are also often focused on meeting the needs of the organization at the expense of the needs of the learner.

A paradigm shift in adult education and training would move from a mechanistic way of seeing the world to more organic and fluid understandings. A possible shift might be to an awareness of the soul of the educator so that renewal and personal energy are seen as possible. The "given" of the field might move to view an adult educator or trainer as a person with vision and with internal knowledge who can help others learn. A second shift might be to see learners as co-participants and subjects of their own learning. In this worldview, the learner and the educator stand in awe of each other as mutually valuable human beings. Such reverence or respect in the learning can become the basis for a paradigm shift to a more spiritually rich education.

*Metaphysical assumptions* are assumptions the educator and learner hold to be real. Adult educators and trainers need to be aware that learners are tuned into the realities of the educational environment and know what is valuable for them. One area is subject matter. Both the learner and the trainer or educator know that to ignore the spiritual component of education is to ignore a very real part of who they are. Neither learners nor educators leave home behind when they enter a designated learning environment. Rigid boundaries between the many worlds within which each participant lives no longer make sense, within a new paradigm.

The denial of a spiritual dimension is fraudulent to the learner. Within adult education and training, a paradigm shift requires addressing relevant issues and situations. Knowing what is real and what is valuable at any given time requires the development and nurturing of discernment. Perhaps the most insightful explanation of discernment and its role in human life comes from Jesuit spirituality (Reiser, 1985). Discernment was a dimension of Jesuit spirituality emphasized by Jesuit founder St. Ignatius of Loyola, who underscored the importance of the discernment of spirits—or sorting out what was evil from what was good. He stressed trusting one's inner feelings and thoughts as indispensable to the discernment process. As Reiser says, "Reading study, thinking, keeping one's mind open to the truth are ingredients of a well-founded spirituality" (p. 136). Discernment is a key process in knowing what is real.

*Value* shifts occur with paradigm shifts. Paradigm shifts encourage a move from what was previously valued to what is now of value. In the case of spirituality, qualities of thinking, feeling, and human will once ignored as part of the educational experience are now a full and integral part of spirituality. Whole person learning is valued because spirituality is not tacked on as a separate learning module. Rather, spirituality is embodied in care and concern for learners, creation of a sacred space for open discussion in the educational environment, and structured experiences that invite learners and educators to ask questions of meaning such as C. Hunt's (1998) question, "Who am I?"

*Exemplars* are needed in the new paradigm to show "people, events and physical symbols that embody the whole approach the paradigm is concerned with" (Vaill, 1998, p. 147). In the case of spirituality and adult education and training, most exemplars come from formal educational institutions. The exemplar we offer here is the California Institute for Integral Studies (2000), San Francisco, which offers graduate level programs in the integration of body/mind/spirit. This institute is an accredited institution that "strives to embody spirit, intellect, and wisdom in service to individuals, communities, and the Earth" (n. p.). The institute lives by seven ideals:

1. The integration of body-mind-spirit

2. Affirmation of spirituality and acknowledgement of spirit as part of the education agenda

3. Commitment to traditions of cultural diversity and to their expression and embodiment throughout all areas

4. Fostering of multiple ways of learning and teaching

5. Advocacy of feminism and sustainability

6. Support of community

7. Active striving for an integral and innovative governance

These ideals provide a blueprint of what spirituallycommitted workplace education programs might try to promote and work towards.

Kuhn's (1970) paradigm shift in the spirituality of adult education and training is in process. We see it in resources already in print, in the attitude of colleagues, and in our own changing and growing conviction that spiritual literacy is an essential part of education. We even see it in the willingness of a publisher to consider publishing a book with the content we have chosen. Publishing, after all, is a pragmatic business. No wise publisher would consider printing a book without a market. Along with our colleagues who call for adult education and training to turn its attention to literacy, numeracy, and cultural literacy, we believe there is room for a spiritual literacy. And, we believe that this spiritual literacy is a full and integral part of whole person learning.

> Developing our ability to visualize and to dream within the context of our everyday lives is just plain hard. Perhaps we can take the example of Chris Cullen (2001), a textile manufacturer and a self-described do it yourselfer (DIYer). Cullen says he finds God in the most mundane of activities—fixing up things around the house or "among the paintbrushes" (p. 24). In realizing that God is not only in creation but in "our creative works" (p. 29), Cullen has come to see his work "in some mysterious way [as] an act of cooperation with the work of God." (p. 29)

## AN ALTERNATIVE VIEW: APPRECIATIVE INQUIRY

Now we look more closely at how the change to a spiritually based adult education and training world might be enabled. We begin by acknowledging that most change models are problem-centered. That is, they are centered on discovering what is wrong in adult education and training, and attempting to address the problems they name. As an alternative to starting with the problems of adult education and training as a way to effect change, we offer another way of effecting a positive vision of the field that is spiritually based. This way has been called appreciative inquiry. Appreciative inquiry has been developed mainly by Cooperrider (Srivastva & Cooperrider, 1999) and his associates at Case Western Reserve University and supported by the research and publication of others, such as Hammond (1998), and Bushe and Pitman (1991).

Appreciative inquiry "takes attention away from problems and deficits and redirects attention to the best of what is" (Lander, 2000a, p. 136). Rather than seeing spirituality as a problem to be solved and a project to be addressed in adult educational and training practice, we agree with Bushe and Pitman's (1991) note that "appreciative inquiry is a way of thinking, seeing and acting for powering transformational change in organizations" (p. 1). As we have noted, appreciative inquiry is not a problem-based orientation that seeks to critique and focus on what is wrong. Most of us know from experience that such "negative" approaches often tend to depress and dedicate themselves to finding problems where, in fact, a circumstance should be best seen for its successes.

Unfortunately, in adult education and training, critique has often meant that researchers come to focus more on lamenting the problem than working on how to fix it. Further, a preoccupation with the deficient can create a climate where people are afraid to try new things for fear of failure and blame. We often read these negative critiques in adult education and training-as we noted with easy historical targets like Malcolm Knowles— wondering if the writer were not more focused on polemic than on research. As we read some of these critiques, we shudder at their arrogance—wondering whether such writers could build a world they could live in. We believe, perhaps because we are teachers, that negative critique stifles creativity and proactivity. Finally, we believe that a problem-solving approach creates a problem-centered educational approach, which can be antithetical to a spiritual education approach.

As a philosophy for change, appreciative inquiry holds exciting possibilities for adult education and training. A similar approach is found in community development with the asset-building strategies of Kretzmann and McKnight (1993). Appreciative inquiry begins with solutions—the solutions that all adult educators and trainers have—the ones they know in their heart of hearts.

In terms of spirituality, this approach assumes that adult educators and trainers and the learners they work with already practice spiritually based approaches, although they may not have been acknowledged or recognized in their work environment by other practitioners. Our challenge is to identify these practices, affirm them, and practice them so that the goal of more fully realizing a vision of spiritually based adult education and training might be reached. In fact, J. A. Neal (2000a) has already made the links between appreciative inquiry and spirituality.

One key concept of appreciative inquiry is that it requires practicing our "appreciative eye," or the ability to find beauty in everything (Hammond, 1998, p. 6). Another key concept is that appreciative inquiry is an integral part of practicing holistic education. To be holistic, adult educators and trainers need to work on looking at the whole of our practice without dissecting each piece looking for what is missing or broken. To find spirituality in adult education and training, practitioners should look for what is already happening that supports spirituality. To help communicate the ideas and practices in appreciative inquiry, Hammond has provided a list of assumptions that support it. These assumptions include (a) in every group or organization, something works; (b) what we focus on becomes our reality; (c) when we ask questions in a group, these questions influence the group; and (d) if we carry parts of the past forward, they should be the best parts (pp. 20–21).

## An Informal Approach to Change

Appreciative inquiry can be fostered in informal ways. Here, we apply two of Bushe and Pitman's (1991) ideas to appreciating spirituality in our educational and training practice. These approaches are called "stalking the flow" and "amplifying through fanning." Stalking the flow refers to looking around for what is working well. Specifically, it includes attending or being mindful to what is already happening in adult education and training programs that supports spirituality. Is a positive climate created in the educational environments? Is there an effort to support the agenda of spirituality?

Bushe and Pitman recommend looking for "life-giving forces" in our places of practice. These life-giving processes "bring out the best in people and the organization" (p. 2). They include respecting and honoring students, creating forums for creative and open discussions, and creating networks of support that contain individual soul friends. Such forces may already be alive and well and help make us effective facilitators of spirituality. However, it is more likely we are not even aware of them.

Stalking the flow allows us to track down the information, people, and ideas in most workplaces that allow us to satisfy our own personal needs. As Bushe and Pitman point out, "an endless stream of problems eventually drains even the most stalwart soul" (p. 2). The focus in appreciative inquiry seeks what is working and what we can affirm to effect positive and spiritual change within an organization.

The second approach Bushe and Pitman recommend is "amplifying through fanning." This means supporting the positive when you see it in the workplace. In terms of spirituality, "fanning" means genuine praise for work well done and blessing of what has already happened that grants people license to continue effective practices. Amplifying the fanning may also mean asking key people in the workplace to support our own work. For example, if we want to support spirituality in our work, we sometimes need key people within the organization to voice support for it. Since we believe that spirituality is best engendered within community, we encourage adult educators or trainers to actively seek to build community. This includes the very difficult task of asking for help. Our experience is that many are willing, but few are asked. Perhaps it is uniquely Western to "go it alone."

We no longer struggle as much with our own pride. Age

has allowed us the insight that others practice spirituality and hospitality through the practice of activity. If we fail to ask, we hurt both ourselves and those who would benefit from the activity of helping—of learning and practicing their own organizational power. We, therefore, encourage adult educators and trainers to ask their colleagues to intervene—to both help and be helped—by those willing to affirm the positive things they are already doing. This may also mean asking others (including leaders within an organization) to intervene and work to remove roadblocks that get in the way.

> *Popular spiritual writer, Hillman (1996) in* The Soul's Code *offers an interesting way of seeing what is inside us, our essence or code. In his "acorn theory of the soul" (p. 11), Hillman argues that each of us has a unique code that we are born with and which is asking to be both lived and uncovered in our own lifetime. It is what makes us unique and human, in search of meaning and of purpose.*

## A Systematic Approach to Appreciative Inquiry

Bushe's and Pitman's (1991) approach to supporting spirituality is mainly informal or casual. As they note, however, to develop their practices, they have drawn on the work of Cooperrider, a practitioner-researcher who developed a more systematic approach to appreciative inquiry. We look now at some possible steps to using this more direct and planned approach to begin valuing and appreciating the existing spiritual dimensions of adult education and training. These steps are drawn from the work of Hammond (1998) and have been adapted here for the change to spiritually based adult education and training.

### Step 1

Having chosen the topic of spirituality, gather people you know are involved with you in the practice of adult education and training. Include learners, educators, staff people, and anyone else involved in your community of practice.

## Step 2

Ask participants these questions or similar ones: Can you recall a special moment when you felt spiritually connected to others in your practice? What about you felt connected? What were you doing? What effect do you feel this had on the people you were working with?

## Step 3

Ask participants these questions or similar ones: Can you recall a special moment of being spiritually grounded in your practice? What was the scenario? Who were the people involved? What factors contributed to your being spiritually grounded?

## Step 4

When these moments have been described, often in vivid detail by participants, and the stories charted on the walls, ask participants to write provocative propositions from the posted data. The next challenge is to find themes or points of convergence in the statements. Ask: Now that you have recorded your stories of your best moments, can you write an affirmative statement that describes your vision of spirituality in adult education? Think about this as speculation about what might be based on the peak moments you have described. Some possible provocative propositions follow:

- We practice positive, respectful, and mutual dialogue with learners.
- We view our community of practice as a safe, inviting place where failure is encouraged.
- We devote time to our spiritual disciplines and practices. We set time aside every day for quiet, reflective activities.
- We work on interconnections and interrelationships through community meals, scheduled meetings, and coffee breaks.
- We practice being mindful with our work.
- We are true to ourselves.

Once propositions have been recorded, Hammond (1998) suggests determining whether they are indeed provocative. Ask:

"Does it stretch, challenge, or innovate?" Other questions might include these: "Is it grounded in examples?" "Will people defend it or get passionate about it?" "Is it stated in affirmative, bold terms and in present tense (as if it were already happening)?" (p. 44).

## Step 5

This step is one of action and innovation, which may not occur right away. Perhaps, it will be part of a growing process for adult educators and trainers. This step can be carried out strategically. The question becomes how we turn our picture or dream for the future into a reality. Adult educators and trainers can make both short-term and long-term plans for the future. The teacher's step is to help ensure that personal and group commitments are part of the plan. Before the process is over, everyone in the group should commit to doing something now to foster the vision of a spiritually based adult education and training.

Of course, we are not naïve about the challenges of using appreciative inquiry. We are aware that, in some ways, appreciative inquiry can become a refusal to look at problems practitioner-researchers may have but that have not been addressed. One problem that immediately comes to mind is the impact of an anti-spiritual leader. However, based on our own experience, we are confident that "problems" like these will surface in the stories of "best moments."

It is inevitable that educators and trainers face roadblocks. However, as Bushe and Pitman (1991) have noted, there are ways around them. Appreciative inquiry does not ignore the roadblocks, but suggests ways to acknowledge but not focus on them. Of course, current educational "tradition" has come to focus on the negative and the desire of some participants will be to focus exclusively on the problems. If possible, these people need reminding that shifting one's attention or way of thinking and speaking is all part of effective appreciative inquiry.

Practicing appreciative inquiry will challenge adult educators and trainers. Still, it holds hope for a more spiritually balanced view and practice. The beauty of the process is that asking appreciative questions seems to touch something deeply important to people. As Hammond (1998) notes, "They give heartfelt answers because we ask soulful questions" (p. 48).

Appreciative inquiry also embodies the essence of a spiritually based adult education and training (Banaga, 1998). It is spiritual because it draws a sense of wonder from the well of what is actually happening spiritually among practitioners and researchers. It attends to things in our work we can be thankful for. Appreciative inquiry is also spiritual because it draws on our sense of hope, our dreams, our visions, and our confidence that better things are to come. This activity is essentially spirit-filled and honors our creativity and our capacity for hope.

Appreciative inquiry is spiritual in that it honors our uniqueness, our diversity, and the fact that each of us has a special, potentially edifying perspective to share. *Edification* comes from the Latin for "to build." What better goal could there be? The diversity of humanity is also an opportunity for greater edification, as we honor the dialogue of participants who strive for common ground. Finally, appreciative inquiry is transformational because it focuses on and actualizes what can and will be. It provides new possibilities for conversion and transformation in the context of adult education and training.

> *Often we search elusively for perfection in ourselves, others, and in our work places. Jean Vanier (1979), French Canadian founder of L'Arche (meaning ark), an international network of homes for people with intellectual disabilities, offers a reminder of the fruitlessness of this search: "It is difficult to make people understand that the ideal doesn't exist, that personal equilibrium and the harmony they dream of come only after years and years of struggle, and that even then they come only as flashes of grace and peace." (p. 17)*

## OUR HOPE FOR CHANGE

Our hope for a changed and more spiritually mature adult education and training field recognizes the beauty of the spiritual dimensions of the practice and the need for an ability to see beauty in our work. We agree with soul writer Sardello (1992) who wonders aloud why the inability to see the beauty of the soul isn't classified as a disease—one he thinks should be called "aesthetic amnesia" (p. 137). What we see as we look at adult education and training is a field in which many practitioner-researchers want to have a closer integration of the spiritual with their practice. What we hope happens is an awakening from the amnesia that seems to have forgotten our heroic past and our heroic quest, pulling together and learning from examples of the past as we shape a critical and spiritual vision for the future.

An example of learning from the past to help shape the future is the work of Bortoft (1986), physicist, philosopher, and professor of the history of science. Bortoft develops the unity we envision in his study of Goethe's (1749–1832) work on scientific consciousness and on the development of new ways to know, see, and value. According to Bortoft, Goethe's scientific method and poetry suggest ways to escape the mechanistic framework of adult education and training. Goethe advocated the cultivation of new faculties of seeing (not unlike the appreciative eye) in which what is being studied is studied as a whole, not as a series of parts. Goethe's concept of *bildung,* or cultivation of faculties, involves paying full attention to the whole so that we and those within our community are transformed. This understanding of how we come to know and how we develop our faculties of perception is the basis of Waldorf education—a broad vision of spirituality not unlike our own. Our hope is that adult education and training begin to attend more closer to the cultivation of faculties of perception, to foster ways of being spiritually grounded, and to practice appreciating what is spiritual in our field.

> *Human beings hold the unique capacity to nurture their spiritual selves, whether they are in religious or sacred places or not. This yearning to be part of a collective and to deepen spirituality is seen in the 200,000 people who go each year to visit Iona, an island community off the*

*coast of Scotland. Iona was the island that St. Columba landed on in 563 C.E. The current spiritual community on the island was formed in 1938. In addition to those who live on the island in the ecumenical community, there are 200 members, 900 associates, and 2000 friends worldwide who are connected by disciplines of prayer and study, and who work for justice and peace. They live in sync with the Iona practices, but from a distance. (Hawn, 2000, pp. 504–505)*

## RESOURCES FOR SPIRITUALITY

We have chosen readings that pay special attention to the spiritual dimension in an educational context. The list is not long because the area is new. Furthermore, because the work is often implicit, it is sometimes difficult to recognize. We may have missed examples that are obvious to others.

Much work still must be done to strengthen the writing and to shore up the theory. (For a further selection of recommended readings, see English & Gillen, 2000a, pp. 89–91). Much of the writing is extremely pro-spirituality and uncritical in its acceptance of the integration of spirituality into professional practice. We also note that little empirical research on spirituality has been done. Because this is true, we encourage our colleagues to read our book, these selections, and investigate the practice we have promoted in this book.

Beauchamp, L., & Parsons, J. (2000). *Teaching from the Inside Out* (3rd ed.). Edmonton, AB: Duval.

This book is an interesting example of how to integrate spiritual ideals within the daily activity of teaching. While it is a practical book, written for teacher candidates at the elementary and secondary level, it differs from other books of its type because it takes an obvious "religious," moral, and spiritual stand. Instead of shying away from the concept of teaching as a vocational enterprise, it presses the vocational call to teaching that motivates most young teachers. The book discusses specific and practical ways teachers can live ethically within the classroom, build moral enduring relationships with those involved in the educational context, and survive in teaching—keeping the faith that first motivated young people to the vocational activity of education. As our friend Bob Patterson, dean of education at Brigham Young University, says, the trust of a child's body and mind is one of the most sacred trusts given in society. The book's third edition is both practical and moral—shaping the two understandings in ways that have, obviously, spoken to teachers. It is written with the "voice" of moral and ethical authority—uncompromising in its belief that there are good things and bad things to do in teaching and that teachers both know and ought to attend to the good. It stands as an interesting example of how the religious/spiritual and the educational can be combined without compromise and apology.

English, L. M., & Gillen, M. A. (Eds.). (2000a). *Addressing the Spiritual Dimensions of Adult Learning: What Educators Can Do.* New Directions for Adult and Continuing Education, No. 85. San Francisco: Jossey-Bass.

Here, English and Gillen have compiled a group of nine essays on various aspects of spirituality and adult education. The authors provide examples of how spirituality has been integrated into areas such as nursing education, higher education, continuing professional education, and First Nations education. The authors discuss issues inherent in integrating spirituality into education, such as the fears educators encounter, the resistance to engage in spiritually based programs, and the struggle to separate religion from spirituality. The authors also identify significant readings and writings related to the spirituality of education, as well as practical advice on how spirituality can be integrated into practice. This is a useful, practical introduction to the spiritual dimensions of adult education.

Fenwick, T. J., & Lange, E. (1998). Spirituality in the workplace: The new frontier of HRD. *Canadian Journal for the Study of Adult Education,* 12 (1), 63–87.

This article, which we have reviewed earlier, provides a critical examination of the integration of spirituality into the workplace. The authors identify the vast explosion of writing on spirituality in the workplace and offer insightful critique that will be useful for adult educators and trainers to read and consider before initiating a spiritually based workplace education program. Fenwick and Lange identify issues such as the different and often conflicting purposes of HRD and spirituality, the fundamentalist zeal of some spirituality initiatives, the potential invasion of personal privacy by the employer, and the resistance to critical discernment. These important issues are carefully considered in the article and are useful for workplace educator.

Hammond, S. A., & Royal, C. (Eds.). (1998). *Lessons from the Field: Applying Appreciative Inquiry.* Plano, TX: Practical Press / Thin Book.

This book is a treasure of vivid, informative case studies and practical ideas about applying appreciative inquiry. Case studies include the application of appreciative inquiry to schools, universities, health care facilities, community development, youth, and international development. The authors also face tough issues, such as how to write a proposal for and introduce appreciative inquiry and how to effect change once the provocative propositions have been written. One of the more useful essays makes explicit connections between spirituality and appreciative inquiry. The author, Banaga, contends that appreciative inquiry is a spiritual approach to change, not merely a method. This book is for those who want to effect change in a way consistent with a spiritual approach to adult education.

Heron, J. (1999). *The Complete Facilitator's Handbook.* London: Kogan Page.

The extremely comprehensive facilitators' guidebook plumbs the depths of facilitation from managing to planning to facilitating. Heron, a practitioner-researcher with 25 years of experience in participatory inquiry, spirituality, and transpersonal psychology, integrates his understandings about spirituality as an integral dimension of whole person learning. Heron is committed to understanding and honoring spirituality and, in true holistic fashion, weaves spiritual themes and ideas through his book, without isolating these. This book is helpful for those wanting to see how spirituality can be interwoven in practice.

Hunt, D. (1992). *The Renewal of Personal Energy.* Toronto: OISE Press.

This book by Ontario Institute for Studies in Education/ University of Toronto professor David Hunt points to the potential of humans to be the source of their own personal renewal. Observing educator stress and burnout, Hunt came to believe that educators best know what they need and how to get it. Hunt shows how learning from experience, especially inner experience, can renew one's personal energy. Pointing to the three R's of renewal: reflexivity, responsivity, and reciprocity, Hunt illustrates how each connects to working from the inside out. This excellent book is useful for adult educators interested in getting in touch with their own personal energy.

Miller, J. P. (2000). *Education and the Soul: Toward a Spiritual Curriculum.* Albany: State University of New York Press.

Miller, a professor of education at the Ontario Institute for Studies in Education/University of Toronto, has written a beautiful book. Miller believes that the educational experience ought to be soulful, that the soul can teach us, and that educators need to bring soul into their practice. One of Miller's key ideas is that educators contribute to this experience by attending deliberately to their own spiritual needs. In describing how we can bring soul into teaching, Miller explores how the soul can be nourished and provides examples and approaches for nurturing the soul in schools and with teachers and students. Miller's own personal case studies and experiences of bringing soul to education make this a worthwhile read for anyone interested in a spiritual curriculum.

Vaill, P. (1998). *Spirited Leading and Learning: Process Wisdom for a New Age.* San Francisco: Jossey-Bass.

This collection of 10 essays is made up of the texts of speeches given by business expert and lecturer Peter Vaill over a 15-year period to a variety of organizational development audiences. The book is divided into four sections: process wisdom, leading, learning, and spirit. Of particular interest to adult educators and trainers are the three essays in the fourth section on spirit. Vaill discusses the place of spirituality in the workplace, even arguing that "any organization, whether it is a global corporation, a huge government agency . . . or just Al and Tony's Auto Body Shop, is a perfectly fine place in which to try to lead a spiritual life" (p. 206). The essays in which he discusses spirituality make it clear he sees spirituality as an integral part of the organizational life. This book is recommended for those in business who have doubts about the place of spirituality in their workplace.

## CONCLUSION

In this book, we have mapped the terrain of spirituality of adult education and training beginning with highlights from the history of the field. We then moved to developing a theoretical basis for spirituality, which allows for critical distinctions in how spirituality is understood and practiced. Having established this groundwork, we offered a practical survey of how to bring spirituality into our personal lives and into our teaching. Workplace education was then selected as a specific site where spirituality might be integrated in a very deliberate way. Finally, in this last chapter we offered adult educators and trainers a framework for change, one that encourages them to spearhead a paradigm shift in thinking about spirituality in our practice. All through this book we have presented stories and nuggets of wisdom from the literature, which we hope will inspire the reader to think more about the ways spirituality is part of the everyday. We challenge you, now that you have finished reading, to begin or to continue practicing spiritual disciplines, allowing you to know the terrain of your own heart and mind more fully, whether it be hilly and rocky or smooth and sandy.

# REFERENCES

Ablom, M. (1997). *Tuesdays with Morrie*. New York: Doubleday.

Apps, J. W. (1996). *Teaching from the heart*. Malabar, FL: Krieger.

Auden, W. H. (1940). In memory of W. B. Yeats. In *Another time*. New York: Random House.

Axel, G. (1989). Babette's feast (Video). (Based on I. Dinesen). New York: Orion Home Video.

Banaga, G. (1998). A spiritual path to organizational renewal. In S. A. Hammond & C. Royal (Eds.), *Lessons from the field: Applying appreciative inquiry*. Plano, TX: Thin Book/Practical Press.

Barnett, R. (1999) Learning to work and working to learn. In D. Boud & J. Garrick, *Understanding learning at work* (pp. 29–44). London: Routledge.

Bass, D. B. (1998). America's trendy look to a feel-good god. *Edmonton Journal*, Saturday, January 10, 1998, p. A14.

Beauchamp, L., & Parsons, J. (2000). *Teaching from the inside out* (3rd ed.). Edmonton, AB: Duval.

Berry, T. (1988). *The dream of the earth*. San Francisco: Sierra Club.

Berthoff, A. E. (1987). Dialectic notebooks and the audit of meaning (pp. 11–32). In T. Fulwiler (Ed.), *The journal book*. Portsmouth, NH: Boynton/Cook.

Billett, S. (2001). Co-participation: Affordance and engagement at work. In T. Fenwick (Ed.), *Sociocultural perspectives on learning through work*. San Francisco: Jossey-Bass. New Directions for Adult and Continuing Education No. 92.

Block, P. (1993). *Stewardship: Choosing service over self-interest*. San Francisco: Berrett-Koehler.

Boal, A. (1998). *Legislative theatre: Using performance to make politics*. (A. Jackson, Trans.). London: Routledge.

Bonhoeffer, D. (1962). *Letters and papers from prison*. (Eberard Bethge, Ed.). New York: Macmillan.

Bortoft, H. (1986) *Goethe's scientific consciousness.* Kent, UK: Institute for Cultural Research.

Boud, D., & Miller, N. (1996). *Working with experience: Animating learning.* New York: Routledge.

Boud, D., & Walker, D. (1998). Promoting reflection in professional courses: The challenge of context. *Studies in Higher Education, 23* (2), 191–206.

Breathnach, S. (1995). *Simple abundance: A daybook of comfort and joy.* New York: Time Warner.

Brockett, R. G. (1990). Adult education: Are we doing it ethically? *MPAEA Journal of Adult Education,* (1), 5–12.

Buber, M. (1958). *I and Thou* (2nd ed.). (R. G. Smith, Trans.) New York: Scribner's.

Buddhaghosa, B. (1976). *The path of purification.* Boston: Shambhala.

Bushe, G., & Pitman, T. (1991). Appreciative process: A method of transformational change. *OD Practitioner,* Sept, 1991, 1–4.

Bynum, C. W. (1987). *Holy feast and holy fast: The religious significance of food to medieval women.* Berkeley: University of California Press.

California Institute for Integral Studies. (2000). Homepage. Available: online at http://www.ciis.edu/welcome/mission.html.

Cameron, J. (1992). *The artist's way: A spiritual path to higher creativity.* New York: Jeremy Tarcher.

Canfield, J., & Hansen, M. V. (1993). *Chicken soup for the soul: 101 stories to open the heart & rekindle the spirit.* Deerfield Beach, FL: Health Communications.

Carrigan, T. (2000). Contemplation versus meditation: What's the difference. Available online at: http://209.1.224.12/Athens/Delphi/5655/essay/medit.html.

Casti, J. L. (1994). *Complexification: Explaining a paradoxical world through the science of surprise.* New York: HarperCollins.

Chia, R. (1997). Process philosophy and management learning: Cultivating 'foresight' in management education. In J. Burgoyne & M. Reynolds (Eds.), *Management learning: Integrating perspectives in theory and practice* (pp. 71–88). London: Sage.

Clark, [M.] C. (1993). Truth, belief and knowledge. In P. Jarvis & N. Walters (Eds.), *Adult education and theological interpretations* (pp. 19–34). Malabar, FL: Krieger.

Clark, M. C. (1999). Challenging the unitary self: Adult education, feminism, and nonunitary subjectivity. *Canadian Journal for the Study of Adult Education, 13* (2) 39–48.

Clark, M. C., & Caffarella, R. S. (Eds.) (1999). Theorizing adult development. In *An update on adult development theory* (pp. 3–8). New Directions for Adult and Continuing Education, No. 84. San Francisco: Jossey-Bass.

Clark, M. C., & Dirkx, J. (2000). Moving beyond the unitary self: a reflective dialogue. In A. L. Wilson & E. R. Hayes (Eds.), *Handbook of adult and continuing education* (pp. 101–116). San Francisco: Jossey-Bass.

Clover, D., Follen, S., & Hall, B. (1998). *The nature of transformation: Environmental, adult and popular education.* Toronto: Transformative Learning Centre.

Coady, M. (1939). *Masters of their own destiny.* New York: Harper & Row.

Cohen, N. H., & Galbraith, M. W. (1995). Mentoring in the learning society. In M. W. Galbraith & N. H. Cohen (Eds.), *Mentoring: New strategies and challenges* (pp. 5–14). New Directions for Adult and Continuing Education, No. 66. San Francisco: Jossey-Bass.

Coles, R. (1990). *The spiritual life of children.* Boston: Houghton Mifflin.

Collins, M. (1991). *Adult education as vocation: A critical role for the adult educator.* New York: Routledge.

Conlin, M. (1999). *Religion in the workplace: The growing presence of spirituality in Corporate America.* Business Week, November 1, 1999. Available online at: http://northernway.org/workplace.html.

Contemplative Outreach (2000). Centering Prayer. Available online at: http://www.centeringprayer.com/.

Cook, G. L. (1987). Educational justice for the campmen: Alfred Fitzpatrick and the foundation of Frontier College, 1899–1922 (pp. 35–51). In M. R. Welton (Ed.), *Knowledge for the people: The struggle for adult learning in English-speaking Canada.* Toronto: OISE Press.

Corbett, E. A. (1952). A. B. MacDonald. In H. Rouillard (Ed.), *Pioneers in adult education in Canada* (pp. 93–99). Toronto: Nelson.

Cullen, C. (2001). Doing it yourself: With God among the paintbrushes. *The Way: Contemporary Christian Spirituality, 41* (1), 24–32.

Daloz, L. (1999). *Mentor guiding the journey of adult learners (2nd ed.).* San Francisco: Jossey-Bass.

Daloz, L. A. P., Keen, C. H., Keen, J. P., & Parks, S. D. (1996). *Common fire: Leading lives of commitment in a complex world.* Boston: Beacon Press.

Darwin, A. (2000). Critical reflections on mentoring in work settings. *Adult Education Quarterly, 50* (3), 197–211.

Davidson, H. R. E. (1988). *Myths and symbols in pagan Europe: Early Scandinavian and Celtic religions.* Syracuse, NY: Syracuse University Press.

Day, D. (1952). *The long loneliness.* New York: Curtis Books.

De Waal, E. (1997). *Celtic light : A tradition rediscovered.* London: Fount.

De Waal, E. (1984). *Seeking God : The way of St. Benedict.* Collegeville, MN: Liturgical Press.

Deane, S. (1977). Scholar II. In *Rumours.* Dublin: Dolmen Press.

Degler, T. (1996). *The fiery muse: Creativity and the spiritual quest.* Toronto: Random House.

Del Prete, T. (1990). *Thomas Merton and the education of the whole person.* Birmingham, AL: Religious Education Press.

Denis, M., & Richter, I. (1987). Learning about intuitive learning: Moose-hunting techniques. (pp. 25–36). In D. Boud & V. Griffin (Eds.), *Appreciating adults learning: From the learners' perspective* (pp. 25–36). London: Kogan Page.

Dewey, J. (1959). My pedagogic creed. In M. S. Dworkin (Intro and notes), *Dewey on Education: Selections.* Classics in Education, No. 3. New York: Teachers College Press. (Originally published 1899).

Dillard, A. (1974). *Pilgrim at Tinker Creek.* New York: Harper's Magazine Press.

Dillard, A. (1982). *Teaching a stone to talk: Expeditions and encounters.* New York: Harper & Row.

Dillard, A. (1984). *Holy the firm.* New York: Harper & Row.

Dillard, C. B., Abdur-Rashid, D. I., & Tyson, C. A. (2000). My soul is a witness: Affirming pedagogies of the spirit. *Qualitative Studies in Education, 13* (5), 447–462.

Dirkx, J. (1997). Nurturing the soul in adult education. In P. Cranton (Ed.). *Transformative learning in action: Insights from practice.* New Directions for Adult and Continuing Education, No. 74. San Francisco: Jossey-Bass.

Dirkx, J. (2000). Spirituality of work: The new opiate or a postmodern search for meaning in life? In C. Symes (Ed.), *Proceedings of Working Knowledge: Productive Learning at Work* (pp. 119–124). Sydney: University of Technology at Sydney.

Driver, T. (1991). *The magic of ritual: Our need for liberating rites that transform our lives and our communities.* HarperSanFrancisco.

Eckhart, M. (1994). *Selected writings.* (O. Davies, Trans.). New York: Penguin Books.

Edwards, R. (1998). Flexibility, reflexivity and reflection in the contemporary workplace. *International Journal of Lifelong Education,* *17* ( 6), 377–388.

Egan, R. J. (1996). New spiritualities require discernment. *Compass,* *14* (2), 6–9.

Elbow, P., & Clark, J. (1987). Desert island discourse: The benefits of ignoring audience. In T. Fulwiler (Ed.), *The journal book.* Portsmouth, NH: Boynton/Cook.

Eliot, T. S. (1944). *Four quartets.* London: Faber and Faber.

Elkins, D. N., Hedstrom, L. J., Hughes, L. L., Leaf, J. A., & Saunders, C. (1988). Toward a humanistic-phenomenological spirituality: Definition, description, and measurement. *Journal of Humanistic Psychology, 28* (4), 5–18.

Elwood, J. M. (2000). Dublin Jesuits create Internet prayer space. *National Catholic Reporter.* April 22, *36* (26), 12–13.

Emblen, J. D. (1992). Religion and spirituality defined according to current use in nursing literature. *Journal of Professional Nursing, 8* (1), 41–47.

English, L. M. (2000a). Alfred North Whitehead, process thought, and the religious education of adults. *Australian Journal of Adult Learning, 40* (2), 66–86.

English, L. M. (2000b). Spiritual dimensions of informal learning. In L. M. English & M. A. Gillen (Eds.), *Addressing the spiritual dimensions of adult learning: What Educators Can Do.* New Directions for Adult and Continuing Education, No. 85. San Francisco: Jossey-Bass.

English, L. M., & Gillen, M. A. (Eds.). (2000a). *Addressing the spiritual dimensions of adult learning: What educators can do.* New Directions for Adult and Continuing Education, No. 85. San Francisco: Jossey-Bass.

English, L. M., & Gillen, M. A. (2000b). A postmodern approach to adult religious education. In A. L. Wilson & E. R. Hayes (Eds.), *Handbook of adult and continuing education.* San Francisco: Jossey-Bass.

English, L. M., & Gillen, M. A. (Eds.). (2001). *Promoting journal writing in adult education.* New Directions for Adult and Continuing Education, No. 90. San Francisco: Josey-Bass.

Fenwick, T. J., & Lange, E. (1998). Spirituality in the workplace: The new frontier of HRD. *Canadian Journal for the Study of Adult Education, 12* (1), 63–87.

Finlayson, D. (1997, February 22). Business consultant preaches happiness: Priest's formula for success, let your people grow. *Edmonton Journal*, p. H4.

Firestone, L. A. (1997). *Awakening Minerva*. New York: Warner Books.

Fisher, J. C. (1997). The social gospel: Lindeman's overlooked inspiration. Paper presented at the Midwest Research to Practice Conference in Adult Continuing and Community Education, Michigan State University, East Lansing, Michigan. October 15-17, 1997. Available online at: http://www.canr.msu.edu/aee/research/fisher.htm.

Flannery, D. D. (2000). Connection. In D. D. Flannery & E. Hayes and Others, *Women as learners: The significance of gender in adult learning* (pp. 111-137). San Francisco: Jossey-Bass.

Foley, G. (1999a). Back to basics: A political economy of workplace change and learning. *Studies in the Education of Adults, 31* (2), 181-96.

Foley, G. (1999b). *Learning in social action: A contribution to understanding informal education*. London: Zed Books.

Fowler, J. W. (1981). *Stages of faith: The psychology of human development and the quest for meaning*. San Francisco: Jossey-Bass.

Fox, M. (1979). *A spirituality named compassion and the healing of the global village, Humpty Dumpty and us*. Minneapolis, MN: Winston Press.

Fox, M. (1983). *Original blessing*. Santa Fe, NM: Bear & Company.

Fox, M. (1994). *The reinvention of work: A new vision of livelihood for our time* (pp. 1-17). HarperSan Francisco.

Frank, D. (1999). *J. B. McLachlan: A biography*. Toronto: James Lorimer.

Freire, P. (1984). Education, liberation and the church. *Religious Education, 19* (4),524-545.

Gaarder, J. (1994). *Sophie's world: A novel about the history of philosophy* (P. Moeller, Trans.). New York: Farrar, Straus, & Giroux.

Gardner, H. (1983). *Frames of mind: The theory of multiple intelligences*. New York: Basic Books.

Garnder, H. (1999). *Intelligence reframed: Multiple intelligences for the 21st century*. New York: Basic Books.

Garrick, J., & Usher, R. (1999). Flexible learning, contemporary work and enterprising selves. *Proceedings of Researching Work and Learning: A First International Conference* (pp. 61-69). School of Continuing Education, University of Leeds, Leeds, UK.

Gehrke, N.J. (1988). On preserving the essence of mentoring as one form of teacher leadership. *Journal of Teacher Education, 39* (1), 43–45.

Gillen, M. (1998). Spiritual lessons from the Antigonish movement. In S. Scott, B. Spencer, & A. Thomas (Eds.), *Learning for life: Canadian readings in adult education* (pp. 273–282). Toronto: Thompson Educational Press.

Glazer, S. (Ed.). (1999). *The heart of learning: Spirituality in education.* New York: Jeremy Tarcher.

Greenleaf, R. K. (1998). *The power of servant-leadership: Essays* (L. C. Spears, Ed.). San Francisco: Berrett-Koehler.

Griffin, D. R. (1988). *Spirituality and society: Postmodern visions.* Albany: State University of New York Press.

Griffin, V. R. (1987). Naming the processes. In D. Boud & V. Griffin (Eds.), *Appreciating adults learning: From the learners' perspective* (pp. 109–221). London: Kogan Page.

Griffin, V. R. (1997). Holistic learning and teaching: Would you play a one-string guitar? (pp. 105–130) In T. Barer-Stein & J. A. Draper (Eds.), *The craft of teaching adults* (2nd ed.). Toronto: Culture Concepts.

Groome, T. H. (1980). *Christian religious education: Sharing our story and vision.* San Francisco: HarperCollins.

Gutierrez, G. (1968). Toward a theology of liberation. In A. Hennelly (Ed.), *Liberation theology: A documentary history* (pp. 62–76). Maryknoll, NY: Orbis.

Hammarskjöld, D. (1964). *Markings* (Leif Sjoberg, Trans.). London: Faber and Faber. (Originally published in 1963)

Hammond, S. A. (1998). *The thin book of appreciative inquiry* (2nd edition). Plano, TX: Thin Book.

Hammond, S. A., & Royal, C. (Eds.). (1998). *Lessons from the field: Applying appreciative inquiry.* Plano, TX: Practical Press/Thin Book.

Hanh, T. N. (1990). *Present moment, wonderful moment: Mindfulness verses for daily living.* Berkeley, CA: Parallax Press.

Harris, M. (1987). Teaching and religious imagination. San Francisco: Harper & Row.

Hart, M. U. (1992). *Working and educating for life: Feminist and international perspectives on adult education.* New York: Routledge.

Havel, V. (1992). On the lookout. *Theosophy, 81* (2) 57.

Havel, V. (1994). MAPS special report: A speech by Vaclav Havel, president of the Czech Republic, Stanford University, Palo Alto, CA,

September 29, 1994. *Newsletter of the Multidisciplinary Association for Psychedelic Studies, 5* (3),Winter 1994–95. Available online at: http://www.maps.org/news-letters/v05n3/05346vac.html

Hawn, C. M. (2000). The wild goose sings: Themes in the worship and music of the Iona Community. *Worship, 74* (6), 504–521.

Healey, C. (1989). *Modern spiritual writers: Their legacies of prayer.* New York: Alba House.

Heron, J. (1998). *Sacred science: Person-centered inquiry into the spiritual and the subtle.* Ross-on-Wye, UK: PCCS Books.

Heron, J. (1999). *The complete facilitator's handbook.* London: Kogan Page.

Heschel, A. J. (1951). *The Sabbath: Its meaning for modern man.* New York: Farrar, Straus & Giroux.

Hickman, M. W. (1999). *A day of rest: Creating a spiritual space in your week.* New York: Avon.

Hildegard of Bingen (1985). Illuminations of Hildegard of Bingen (M. Fox, commentator ). Sante Fe, NM: Bear & Co.

Hildegard of Bingen (1987). *Book of divine works with letters and songs* (M. Fox, Ed., intro.). Sante Fe, NM: Bear & Co.

Hillesum, E. (1985). *An interrupted life: The diaries of Etty Hillesum 1941–43.* New York: Washington Square Press.

Hillman, J. (1996). *The soul's code: In search of character and calling.* New York: Random House.

Hogan, C. (1994). Empowering ethical endings. *Management Development Review, 7* (1), 32–40.

hooks, b. (1999). Embracing freedom: Spirituality and liberation. In S. Glazer (Ed.), *The heart of learning: Spirituality in education* (pp. 113–129). New York: Jeremy Tarcher.

Hughes, K., & Quinn, B. (1993). The transfer and the RCIA: Process and ritual. *Review for Religious, 52* (1), 91–92.

Hunt, C. (1998). An adventure: From reflective practice to spirituality. *Teaching in Higher Education, 3* (3), 325–337.

Hunt, D. (1992). *The renewal of personal energy.* Toronto: OISE Press.

Iannone, R. V., & Obenauf, P. A. (1999, summer). Toward spirituality in curriculum and teaching. *Education, 119,* 737–745.

Imel, S. (1998). Spirituality in the workplace. ERIC Trends and Issues Alerts. Retrieved from http://ericave.org. ERIC Clearinghouse on Adult, Career, and Vocational Education. ED 420789.

Jager, W. (1995). *Search for the meaning of life: Essays and reflections on the mystical experience.* Ligouri, MI: Triumph Books.

Jarvis, P., & Walters, N. (Eds.). (1993). *Adult education and theological interpretations*. Malabar, FL: Krieger.

Jones, L. B. (1996). *The path: Creating your mission statement for work and for life*. New York: Hyperion.

*Journal of Bodywork and Movement Therapies. 3* (2), 107–117.

Julian of Norwich. (1978). *Showings*. (E. Colledge & J. Walsh, Series Eds.). Classics of Western Spirituality series. New York: Toronto: Paulist Press.

Kavafy, C. (1989). Ithaca. In *With Ithaca on my mind: An anthropologist's journey* (Lambros Comitas, Trans.). New York: Teachers College, Columbia University.

Kennedy, W. B. (1981). Highlander praxis: Learning with Myles Horton. *Teachers College Record, 83* (1), 105–119.

Kessler, R. (2000). *The soul of education: Helping students find connection, compassion, and character at school*. Alexandria, VA: Association for Supervision and Curriculum Development.

Kleiner, A. (1996). *The age of heretics, heroes, outlaws and the forerunners of corporate change*. New York: Doubleday.

Knowles, M. S. (1962). *The adult education movement in the United States*. New York: Holt, Rinehart, and Winston.

Koch, C. (1990). "Foreword" to P. M. Vinje, *Praying with Catherine of Sienna* (pp. 7–12). Winona, MN: Saint Mary's Press.

Kretzmann, J. P., & McKnight, J. L. (1993). *Building communities from the inside out: A path toward finding and mobilizing a community's assets*. Chicago: ACTA Publications.

Krieger, D. (1993). *Accepting your power to heal: The personal practice of therapeutic touch*. Santa Fe, NM: Bear & Company.

Kuhn, T. S. (1970). *The structure of scientific revolutions*. Chicago: University of Chicago Press.

Kung, H. (1988). *Theology for the third millennium. An ecumenical view*. New York: Doubleday.

Lander, D. A. (2000a). A provocation: Quality is service. *Quality in Higher Education, 6* (2), 135–142.

Lander, D. A. (2000b). Women's Christian Temperance Union. Proceedings of the AERC conference, Vancouver, BC, Canada, June 2–4.

Lange, E. (1998). Fragmented ethics of justice: Freire, liberation theology and pedagogies for the non-poor. *Convergence, 21* (1 &2), 81–94.

Lawler, P. A. (2000). Ethical issues in continuing professional education. In V. Mott & B. J. Daley (Eds.), *Charting a course of continuing professional education: Reframing professional practice* (pp. 63–70). New Directions for Adult and Continuing Education, No. 86. San Francisco: Jossey-Bass.

Lee, C., & Zemke, R. (1993). The search for spirit in the workplace. *Training, 30* (6), 21–28.

Leech, K. (1977). *Soul friend: A study of spirituality.* London: Sheldon Press.

Leigh, P. (1997, March). The new spirit at work. *Training and Development,* 26–33.

L'Engle, M. (1993). *The rock that is higher.* Wheaton, IL: Harold Shaw Publishers.

Levinson, D. J. et al. (1978). *Seasons of a man's life.* New York: Knopf.

Lindeman, E. C. (1921). *The community: An introduction to the study of community leadership and organization.* New York: Association Press.

Livingstone, D. W. (1998). *The education—jobs gap: Underemployment or economic democracy.* Toronto: Garamond Press.

Lonergan, B. (1957). *Insight.* London: Longmans, Green.

MacAulay, K., Hynes, T., Mahaffey, T., & Wright, B. (2000, June). Toward a theoretical model of student spirituality in higher education. Paper presented at the Society of Teaching and Learning in Higher Education. St. Catherine's, ON.

Mack, J. E. (1992). Psychoanalysis of the self: Toward a spiritual point of view. In L. S. Rouner (Ed.), *Selves, people, and persons: What does it mean to be a self?* (pp. 169–186). Notre Dame, IN: University of Notre Dame Press.

MacKeracher, D. M. (1996). *Making sense of adult learning.* Toronto: Culture Concepts.

MacLeod, G. (1997). *From Mondragon to America: Experiments in community economic development.* Sydney, NS: Canada: University College of Cape Breton Press.

MacPherson, S. (1996). The adulthood of Buddhahood: Buddhism, lifelong learning and the education of desire. *International Journal of Lifelong Education, 15* (6), 455–470.

Marcel, G. (1949). *The philosophy of existence.* New York: Philosophical Library.

McMillen, K. (1993). *When the canary stops singing.* San Francisco: Berret-Koehler.

McNeill, J. (April 14, 2000). As my body grows older my spirit becomes younger. *National Catholic Reporter.* Excerpt from his book,

(1998) *Both feet firmly planted in midair: My spiritual journey.*
Westminster John Knox Press. Louisville, KY:

Mechthild of Magdeburg. (1991). *Flowing light of the divinity* (Christiane Mesch Galvani, Trans.). (Susan Clark, Ed., intro.). Garland Library of Medieval Literature, No. 72, Series B. New York: Garland.

Melamed, L. (1987). The role of play in adult learning. In D. Boud & V. Griffin (Eds.), *Appreciating adults learning* (pp. 13–24). London: Kogan Page.

Merriam, S. B., & Heuer, B. (1996). Meaning-making, adult learning and development: A model with implications for practice. *International Journal of Lifelong Education, 15* (4), 243–255.

Miller, J. P. (1993). *The holistic teacher.* Toronto: OISE Press.

Miller, J. P. (2000). *Education and the soul: Toward a spiritual curriculum.* Albany: State University of New York Press.

Mills, N., Allen, J., & Morgan, S. C. (2000). Does Tai Chi/Qi Gong help patients with multiple sclerosis? *Journal of Bodywork and Movement Therapies* 4(1), 39–48.

Mitroff, I., & Denton, E. A. (1999). *A spiritual audit of corporate America: A hard look at spirituality, religion, and values in the workplace.* San Francisco: Jossey-Bass.

Mitton, M. (1996). *The soul of Celtic spirituality in the lives of its saints.* Mystic, CN: Twenty-Third Publications.

Moore, T. (1994). *Care of the soul: A guide for cultivating depth and sacredness in everyday life.* New York: HarperPerennial.

Moules, N.J. (2000). Postmodernism and the sacred: Reclaiming connection in our greater than human worlds. *Journal of Marital and Family Therapy* 26 (2), 229–240.

Nadesan, M. H. (1999). The discourses of corporate spiritualism and evangelical capitalism. *Management Communication Quarterly, 13* (1), 3–42.

Neal, J. A. (1997). Spirituality in management education: A guide to resources. *Journal of Management Education, 21* (1), 121–139.

Neal, J. A. (2000a). Bibliography. Available online at: www. spiritatwork.ca.

Neal, J. A. (2000b). Spiritual evolution. Available online at: www. spiritatwork.com.

Neal, J. A. (2000c).Work as service to the divine: Giving our gifts selflessly and with joy. *American Behavioral Scientist, 43* (8), 1316–1333.

Neal, R. (1998). *Brotherhood economics: Women and co-operatives in Nova Scotia.* Sydney, NS: UCCB Press.

Newman, M. (1999). *Maeler's regard: Images of adult learning.* Sydney, Australia: Stewart Victor.

Norris, K. (1996). *The cloister walk.* New York: Riverhead Books.

Nouwen, H. (1986). *Lifesigns.* New York: Doubleday.

O'Brien, J. (1985). Eastern spirituality and the religious educator. In J. M. Lee (Ed.), *The spirituality of the religious educator* (pp. 170–189). Birmingham, AL; Religious Education Press.

Oliver, H. H. (1992). The relational self. In L. S. Rouner (Ed.), *Selves, people, and persons: What does it mean to be a self?* (pp. 37–51). Notre Dame, IN: University of Notre Dame Press.

Ó Murchú, D. (1998). *Reclaiming spirituality.* New York: Crossroad.

Orr, J. A. (2000). Learning from native adult education. In L. M. English & M. A. Gillen (Eds.), *Addressing the spiritual dimensions of adult learning: What educators can do.* New Directions for Adult and Continuing Education, No. 85 San Francisco: Jossey-Bass.

Palmer, P. (1983). *To know as we are known: A spirituality of education.* New York: HarperCollins.

Palmer, P. (1998). *The courage to teach.* San Francisco: Jossey-Bass.

Palmer, P. (2000). *Let your life speak: Listening for the voice of vocation.* San Francisco: Jossey-Bass.

Parsons, J., & Beauchamp, L. (1991). *Stories of teaching.* Richmond Hill, ON: Scholastic.

Pierce, G. F. A. (1999). Let's create a spirituality of work that works. *US Catholic, 64* (9), 24.

Pierce, G. F. A. (2000). *Spirituality @ work: 10 ways to balance your life on-the-job.* Chicago: Loyola Press.

*The pilgrim continues his way.* (1986). (R. M. French, Trans.). London: Triangle. (Originally published 1943)

Pinar, W., Reynolds, P., & Taubman, P. (1995). *Understanding curriculum: An introduction to the study of historical and contemporary curriculum discourses.* New York: P. Lang.

Principe, W. (1997). Aquinas' spirituality for Christ's faithful living in the world. *Spirituality Today, 44* (2), 110–131.

Progoff, I. (1992). *At a journal workshop: Writing to access the power of the unconscious and evoke creative ability* (Rev. ed.). New York: Jeremy Tarcher.

Purpel, (1989). *The moral and spiritual crisis in education: A curriculum for justice and compassion in education.* New York: Bergin & Garvey.

Redfield, J. (1993). *The Celestine prophecy.* New York: Warner.

Reiser, W. E. (1985). Jesuit spirituality and the religious educator. In J. M. Lee (Ed.), *The spirituality of the religious educator* (pp. 124–149). Birmingham, AL: Religious Education Press.

Rilke, R. M. (1984). Letter 4, *Letters to a young poet* (Stephen Mitchell, Trans.). New York: Random House.

Rolph, J. (1991). Can there be quality in teacher education without spirituality? *Assessment and Evaluation in Higher Education, 16* (1), 49–55.

Roth, N. (2001). Close to God's heart in the garden. *The Way: Contemporary Christian Spirituality, 41* (1), 33–41.

Rouillard, H. (Ed.). (1952). *Pioneers in adult education in Canada.* Toronto: Nelson.

Sardello, R. (1992). *Facing the world with soul.* Hudson, NY: Lindisfarne Press.

Schulz, S. F. (1995). The benefits of mentoring. In M. W. Galbraith & N. Cohen (Eds.), *Mentoring: New strategies and challenges.* New Directions for Adult and Continuing Education, No. 66 (pp. 57–68). San Francisco: Jossey-Bass.

Secretan, L. H. K. (1996). *Reclaiming higher ground: Creating organizations that inspire the soul.* Toronto: Macmillan.

Sellner, E. C. (1990). *Mentoring: The ministry of spiritual kinship.* Notre Dame, IN: Ave Maria Press.

Selman, G. (1998). Issues in adult education. Program No. 9. Videotape. Vancouver: Continuing Studies, University of British Columbia.

Shankar, R. (2000). Nada Brahma — sound is god. Available online at: http://www.ravishankar.org/foundation_frame.html

Shorto, R. (1997, Dec. 7). Belief by the numbers. *New York Times Magazine,* Section 6, pp. 60–61, 114.

Silandanda, U. (1990). *The four foundations of mindfulness.* Boston: Wisdom Publications.

Slattery, P. (1995). *Curriculum development in the postmodern era.* New York: Garland.

Smith, J. (1985). Ecumenical spirituality and the religious educator. In J. M. Lee (Ed.), *The spirituality of the religious educator* (pp. 88–105). Birmingham, AL; Religious Education Press.

Solomon, N. (1998). Culture and difference at work. In D. Boud & J. Garrick (Eds.), *Understanding learning at work* (pp. 119–131). New York and London: Routledge.

Spretnak, C. (1991). *States of grace: The recovery of meaning in the postmodern age.* HarperSanFrancisco.

Srivastva, S., & Cooperrider, D. L. (1999). *Appreciative management and leadership: The power of positive thought and action in organization* (2nd ed.). Euclid, OH: Williams Custom Publishing.

Taylor, C. (1996). Spirituality of life—and its shadow. *Compass,* 14 (2), 10–13.

Teresa of Avila. (1946). *The complete works of Saint Teresa of Jesus* (E. Allison Peers, Trans.). 3 vols. London: Sheed & Ward.

Tisdell, E. J. (1999a). The spiritual dimension of adult development. In C. Clark & R. Caffarella (Eds.), *Adult development: An update.* New Directions for Adult and Continuing Education, No. 84. San Francisco: Jossey-Bass.

Tisdell, E. J. (1999b). Women teaching for social change in adult education: The spiritual and cultural dimensions of "teaching across borders." Paper presented at the Adult Education Research Conference. DeKalb: Northern Illinois University.

Tisdell, E. J. (2000a). Feminist pedagogies. In D. Flannery & E. Hayes and Others, *Women as Learners* (pp. 155–183). San Francisco: Jossey-Bass.

Tisdell, E. J. (2000b). Spirituality and emancipatory adult education in women adult educators for social change. *Adult Education Quarterly, 50* (4), 308–335.

Usher, R., Bryant, I., & Johnston, R. (1997). *Adult education and the postmodern challenge.* London: Routledge.

Vaill, P. (1998). *Spirited leading and learning: Process wisdom for a new age.* San Francisco: Jossey-Bass.

Van den Blink, A. J. (1999). Reflections on spirituality in Anglican theological education. *Anglican Theological Review, 81* (3), 429–449.

Vanier, J. (1979). *Community and growth: Our pilgrimage together.* Toronto: Griffin House.

Vella, J. (2000). A spirited epistemology: honoring the adult learner as subject. In L. M. English & M. A. Gillen (Eds.), *Addressing the spiritual dimensions of adult learning: What educators can do* (pp. 7–16). New Directions for Adult and Continuing Education, No. 85. San Francisco: Jossey-Bass.

Ver Beek, K. A. (2000). Spirituality: A development taboo. *Development in Practice, 10* (1), 31–43.

Vinje, P. M. (1990). *Praying with Catherine of Sienna.* Winona, MN: Saint Mary's Press.

Vogel, L. J. (2000). Reckoning with the spiritual lives of adult educators. In L. M. English & M. A. Gillen (Eds.), *Addressing the spiritual dimensions of adult learning: What educators can do* (pp. 17–27). New Directions for Adult and Continuing Education, No. 85. San Francisco: Jossey-Bass.

Waldrop, M. M. (1992). *Complexity: The emerging science at the edge of order and chaos.* New York: Simon & Schuster.

Walters, S., & Manicom, L. (Eds.). (1996). Introduction. In *Gender in popular education: Methods for empowerment* (pp. 1–22). London: Zed books.

Ward, B. B. (Trans.). (1975). *The sayings of the Desert Fathers: The alphabetical collection.* Cistercian Studies Series, No. 59. London: Mowbrays.

Welton, M. R. (Ed.). (1987). *Knowledge for the people: The struggle for adult learning in English-speaking Canada.* Toronto: OISE Press.

Welton, M. R. (1991). *Toward developmental work: The workplace as a learning environment.* Victoria, Australia: Deakin University.

Welton, M. R. (1993). Seeing the light: Christian conversion and con-scientization. In P. Jarvis & N. Walters (Eds.), *Adult education and theological interpretations* (pp.105–123). Malabar, FL: Krieger.

Whitehead, A. N. (1929). *Process and reality: An essay in cosmology.* New York: Macmillan.

Whitehead, E. E., & Whitehead, J. D. (1995). *Seasons of strength: New visions of adult Christian maturing.* Winona, MN: Saint Mary's Press.

Whitehead, J. D., & Whitehead, E. E. (1994). *Shadows of the heart: A spirituality of the negative emotions.* New York: Crossroad.

Wilber, K. (1997). *The eye of spirit: An integral vision for a world gone slightly mad.* Boston: Shambhala.

Williamson, M. (1993). *A return to love: Reflections on the principles of a course in miracles.* New York: HarperPaperbacks.

Wilson, A. (Ed.). (1991). *World's scripture: A comparative anthology of sacred texts.* International Religious Foundation. Available online at: http://www.unification.net/ws/theme124.htm.

Wiltz, T. (1997). The mystical world of Kabbalah: Trendy seek instant kharma via ancient tradition of Jerusalem. *Edmonton Journal,* Saturday, August 16, 1997, p. G4.

Wlodkowski, R. J. (1999). *Enhancing adult motivation to learn: A comprehensive guide for teaching all adults* (Rev. ed.). San Francisco: Jossey-Bass.

Wuthnow, R. (1998). *After heaven: Spirituality in America since the 1950s.* Berkley: University of California Press.

Yeaxlee, B. (1925). *Spiritual values in adult education* (2 vols.). London: Oxford University Press.

Zachary, L. J. (2000). *The mentor's guide*. San Francisco: Jossey-Bass.

Zinn, L. M. (1997). Spirituality in adult education. *Adult Learning, 8* (5 & 6), 26–30.

Zohar, D., & Marshall, I. N. (2000). *SQ: Spiritual intelligence*. London: Bloomsbury.

Zukav, G. (1990). *The seat of the soul*. New York: Simon & Schuster.

# INDEX